GRAN CANARIA TRAVEL GUIDE

Discover Hidden Gems & Unforgettable Experiences
This Enchanted Island

Clemente Rivera

All rights reserved. No part of this book may be reproduced, stored in a retrieval system, or transmitted in any form or by any means, electronic, mechanical, photocopying, recording, or otherwise, without the prior written permission of the copyright owner. The information contained in this book is for general information purposes only. The author and publisher make no representations or warranties of any kind, express or implied, about the completeness, accuracy, reliability, suitability or availability with respect to the book or the information, products, services, or related graphics contained in the book for any purpose. Any reliance you place on such information is therefore strictly at your own risk.

Copyright © 2024 by Clemente Rivera.

TABLE OF CONTENT

Introduction 8
    Welcome to Gran Canaria 8
    Why Gran Canaria: 9

Part 1: Planning Your Gran Canaria Escape 12
    When to Visit and Weather Conditions 12
    Visas & Entry Requirements 15
    Packing Essentials 17
    Trip Planning Tools and Resources 19
    Where to Stay in Gran Canaria 21

Part 2: Unveiling Gran Canaria's Treasures 36
    Top Tourist Attractions & Activities 36
    Las Palmas: Unveiling the vibrant capital city 44
    Unveiling the Island's Diverse Landscapes: 55
    Exploring the Coast: 61
    Adventure Activities: Hiking, cycling, water sports, and exploring hidden gems 65

Part 3: Tantalize Your Taste Buds: Gran Canaria's Culinary Delights 70
    A Gastronomic Journey: Exploring Local Cuisine 70
    Best Local Drinks to Savor 73
    Street Food and Markets: 76
    Top Restaurants in Gran Canaria 80
    Nightlife: Bars, Pubs, and Clubs 85

Part 4: Exploring Gran Canaria: Itineraries for Every Traveler 92
    Outdoor Adventure Itinerary (hiking, cycling, exploring natural wonders) ... 92

- Romantic Getaway Itinerary 96
- Coastal Relaxation Itinerary 101
- Budget-Friendly Itinerary 105
- Historical and Cultural Immersion Itinerary 111
- Art and Architecture Delights 116
- Family Fun Itinerary 122
- Festivals and Events: Celebrating Gran Canaria's Spirit 128

Part 6: Beyond the Tourist Trail: Unforgettable Experiences 136
- Hidden Gems & Lesser-Known Destinations: 136
- Outdoor Activities & Adventures 140
- Fun Things to Do During Your Visit 145

Part 7: Practical Information for a Smooth Journey 152
- Safety and Security Considerations 152
- Transportation & Getting Around 153
- Money Matters and Currency Exchange 155
- Emergency Contact Numbers 157
- Tourist Traps to Avoid (tips for navigating scams and maximizing your travel budget) 159

Conclusion 164

DISCLAIMER!!!

Welcome to your Gran Canaria adventure! We're thrilled to be your travel companion as you explore this vibrant Destination.

You might have noticed this guide is packed with information but light on pictures. We made a conscious decision to focus on the written word for a few reasons:

- **Unleashing Your Imagination:** We believe the power of imagination is a key ingredient in travel. Detailed descriptions allow you to paint your own mental picture of Galapagos Island's charming streets, mouthwatering food, and breathtaking views.
- **Focus on the Details:** Sometimes, a photo can't capture the essence of a place. We wanted to delve deeper, providing insightful details you might miss in a quick glance at an image. Imagine the scent of freshly baked Pastel de Nata wafting from a bakery, or the sounds of lively conversation echoing through a Fado house - these details come alive through words.
- **A Lighter Carry-On:** Let's face it, travel guides can get heavy! By skipping the photos, we've kept this guide nice and compact, making it easier to slip into your backpack and explore the city hands-free.

Of course, the beauty of Gran Canaria is best experienced firsthand. This guide is here to equip you with the knowledge and inspiration to create unforgettable memories. So, put on your walking shoes, grab your trusty guide, and get ready to fall in love with Gran Canaria!

SCAN CODE TO VIEW MAP OF GRAN CANARIA

Introduction

Welcome to Gran Canaria

Imagine yourself stepping off the plane and being greeted by a warm Canarian breeze carrying the scent of sun-drenched beaches and volcanic earth. Vivid bougainvillea cascades over whitewashed houses, painting the scene with vibrant colors. The distant rumble of the ocean mingles with the joyful chatter of locals, and a sense of serenity washes over you. This is Gran Canaria, a captivating island paradise waiting to be explored.

Gran Canaria isn't just another beach destination. It's a place where dramatic volcanic landscapes cradle pristine beaches, charming villages whisper tales of a rich history, and the spirit of fiesta fills the air with infectious energy. Whether you're a sun-worshipper seeking endless stretches of golden sand, an adventurer yearning to conquer volcanic peaks, or a culture enthusiast captivated by ancient traditions, Gran Canaria has something to ignite your wanderlust.

Prepare to be swept away by the island's dramatic topography. Hike through verdant valleys carved by ancient volcanic eruptions, and witness the majestic Pico de las Nieves, Gran Canaria's highest peak, often veiled by wispy clouds. Explore hidden coves accessible only by foot, where turquoise waters lap at secluded beaches, offering a haven of tranquility.

Immerse yourself in the vibrant capital city, Las Palmas de Gran Canaria. Wander through the charming Vegueta district, a UNESCO World Heritage Site, where colonial architecture whispers stories of conquest and exploration. Meander along the lively Las Canteras beach promenade, a melting pot of locals and visitors soaking up the sunshine. Explore bustling markets overflowing with fresh, local produce, and savor the island's delectable cuisine on a cozy restaurant terrace overlooking the sparkling harbor.

Gran Canaria's allure extends beyond the obvious. Venture into the island's heart and discover charming whitewashed villages nestled amidst rolling hills. Time seems to slow down as you stroll cobblestone streets adorned with colorful flower pots, and the warm smiles of friendly locals make you feel instantly welcome. In these hidden gems, you'll find a glimpse into Gran Canaria's rich cultural tapestry, where ancient traditions are still celebrated with fervor.

Get ready to be captivated by the island's infectious energy. Witness the vibrant Carnival celebrations, a riot of colors, costumes, and music that pulsates through the streets. Immerse yourself in the rhythmic beats of local music during a lively "romería" (pilgrimage) or lose yourself in the electrifying atmosphere of a traditional Canarian fiesta, where locals and visitors come together to celebrate life under the starlit sky.

Gran Canaria is an island that stays with you long after you depart. It's a place where the warmth of the sun meets the coolness of volcanic rock, where the taste of fresh seafood lingers on your palate, and the echo of laughter from a lively fiesta fills your heart with joy. So, pack your bags, embrace the spirit of adventure, and prepare to be captivated by the magic of Gran Canaria!

Why Gran Canaria:

Imagine yourself sinking your toes into warm, golden sand, the turquoise ocean lapping gently at your feet. A gentle breeze carries the scent of salt and exotic flowers, while the vibrant buzz of a happy holiday destination fills the air. This isn't just a daydream; it's the reality waiting for you in Gran Canaria, a captivating island paradise nestled in the Atlantic Ocean.

But Gran Canaria offers so much more than just picture-perfect beaches. This diverse island boasts a unique charm that will captivate your senses and leave you yearning to return. Let me share a glimpse of the magic that awaits:

- **Beaches for Every Mood:** Imagine long stretches of golden sand, perfect for sunbathing and soaking up the Canarian sunshine. Picture secluded coves with crystal-clear waters, ideal for snorkeling and exploring the vibrant underwater world. Gran Canaria caters to every beach desire, from the lively shores of Playa del Inglés to the serene beauty of Playa de Mogán.
- **Volcanic Wonders:** Journey beyond the beaches and discover the island's dramatic volcanic origins. Hike through the lunar landscapes of Fataga Natural Park, where volcanic craters and rugged terrain create a breathtaking backdrop for exploration. Venture to the Roque Nublo, a majestic volcanic rock formation that pierces the sky, offering panoramic views that will leave you speechless.
- **A Tapestry of Cultures:** Gran Canaria's rich history is woven into the very fabric of the island. Explore the charming old town of Las Palmas, where colonial architecture whispers tales of Spanish conquistadors. Immerse yourself in the vibrant culture of the Canarian people, where ancient traditions blend seamlessly with modern life. Witness the colorful displays of Carnival, a celebration of joy and exuberance, or lose yourself in the rhythmic beats of local music during a traditional fiesta.
- **A Foodie Paradise:** Get ready to tantalize your taste buds! Gran Canaria's cuisine is a delicious fusion of Spanish and Canarian influences, with fresh seafood taking center stage. Savor the melt-in-your-mouth "papas arrugadas" (wrinkled potatoes) with mojo sauce, a local specialty. Indulge in a plate of "ropa vieja" (shredded beef stew), a dish bursting with flavor. Don't forget to sample the locally produced wines, the perfect accompaniment to any meal.
- **Adventure Awaits:** Thrill-seekers, rejoice! Gran Canaria offers a plethora of adventure activities to get your adrenaline pumping. Hike through breathtaking trails, challenge yourself with a mountain bike ride through challenging terrain, or feel the exhilaration of windsurfing across the waves. For a unique experience, explore hidden caves with a guided tour, or go spelunking and discover the island's subterranean secrets.

These are just a taste of the captivating charm that awaits you in Gran Canaria. Whether you seek relaxation under the sun, exploration of dramatic landscapes, or immersion in a vibrant culture, this island paradise has something for everyone. So, pack your bags, embrace the spirit of adventure, and get ready to experience the magic of Gran Canaria!

Part 1: Planning Your Gran Canaria Escape

When to Visit and Weather Conditions

Ah, Gran Canaria! The very name conjures images of sun-drenched beaches, crystal-clear waters, and endless summer days. But before you pack your swimsuit and head straight for the airport, let's delve into the island's weather secrets to ensure your trip coincides with the perfect conditions for your dream vacation.

Sunshine All Year Round: A Canary Island Advantage

Gran Canaria, blessed by its subtropical location off the coast of Africa, boasts sunshine almost year-round. This means you can escape the chill of winter in Europe and bask in pleasant temperatures even in December. However, there are subtle variations throughout the year, impacting not only the temperature but also the crowds and overall vibe.

Spring Symphony: Ideal for Hikers and Budget Travelers (March-May)

Spring paints Gran Canaria in vibrant hues. Wildflowers carpet the mountainsides, and the island awakens from its winter slumber. Temperatures hover around a comfortable 20°C (68°F), perfect for outdoor exploration. Hiking trails come alive with blooming vegetation, and the crowds haven't reached their peak yet. This makes spring an ideal time for budget-conscious travelers who can snag good deals on flights and accommodations. However, be prepared for occasional bursts of rain, especially in April and May. Pack a light rain jacket just in case!

Summer Sizzle: Beach Bums Paradise (June-August)

Buckle up for sunshine overload! Summer in Gran Canaria is all about soaking up the sun on pristine beaches. Temperatures soar to a delightful 26°C (79°F), with minimal rainfall. This is peak season for tourism, so expect lively resorts, bustling beaches, and vibrant nightlife. If you crave a quintessential beach vacation with endless sunbathing, snorkeling, and water sports, summer is your time to shine. However, be prepared for slightly higher prices and larger crowds.

Autumn's Golden Touch: A Tranquil Escape (September-November)

As summer wanes, Gran Canaria gracefully transitions into autumn. The scorching sun mellows down to a pleasant 23°C (73°F), offering the perfect blend of warmth and comfort. The crowds start to thin out, creating a more relaxed and tranquil atmosphere. This makes autumn ideal for travelers seeking a peaceful escape, a romantic getaway, or exploring the island's cultural side without battling the crowds. Be aware that while rain is still infrequent, there's a slightly higher chance of encountering a passing shower.

Winter Wonderland (Gran Canaria Style): Mild Temperatures and Festive Cheer (December-February)

While most of Europe shivers under snow, Gran Canaria enjoys what might seem like an eternal spring. Temperatures dip slightly to a still-pleasant 18°C (64°F). This makes winter a fantastic time for sightseeing and exploring the island's charming towns and villages. Plus, the festive spirit comes alive as Christmas markets and New Year's celebrations infuse the island with a magical ambiance. However, keep in mind that the wind can pick up a bit during this time, making the northern coast slightly cooler. Pack a light sweater and a windbreaker to adapt to the occasional breeze.

Choosing Your Perfect Season: Matching Your Interests with the Island's Charm

Ultimately, the ideal time to visit Gran Canaria depends on your travel desires.

- **Beach Bums:** Craving endless sun and sizzling temperatures? Aim for June-August.
- **Budget Backpackers:** Score good deals on flights and accommodations during the shoulder seasons (spring and autumn).
- **Hiking Enthusiasts:** Enjoy the blooming landscapes and comfortable hiking temperatures of spring (March-May).
- **Culture Connoisseurs:** Escape the crowds and immerse yourself in the island's history and traditions during the tranquil autumn months (September-November).
- **Romantic Rendezvous:** Seek a peaceful getaway with mild temperatures and charming festive vibes during winter (December-February).

Beyond the Averages: Microclimates and the Importance of Location

Remember, Gran Canaria boasts diverse microclimates. The southern regions tend to be drier and sunnier all year round, while the north experiences slightly more rain and cooler temperatures. Even within a single day, you might encounter variations – the mornings can be pleasantly cool on the coast but delightfully warm further inland.

Insider Tip: Consider your accommodation's location when planning your trip. If sunshine is your top priority, choose the south. If you prefer cooler temperatures and don't mind the occasional cloud, the north offers a lusher landscape and breathtaking mountain views.

By understanding Gran Canaria's weather patterns and the unique charm of each season, you can tailor your trip to perfectly match your travel dreams. Let this be the first step on your unforgettable Gran Canaria adventure!

Visas & Entry Requirements

Imagine the anticipation bubbling over as you book your flight to Gran Canaria. Pristine beaches beckon, volcanic landscapes whisper tales of ancient eruptions, and delicious local cuisine tantalizes your taste buds. But before you get swept away in the daydream, there's one essential hurdle: visas and entry requirements. Fear not, fellow traveler, for this chapter will be your friendly guide through the process.

Smooth Sailing for Most: The Visa-Free Entry

The good news is that entry into Gran Canaria, and Spain in general, is fairly straightforward for citizens of most European Union countries, the United States, Canada, Australia, and New Zealand. If you fall into this category, congratulations! You can typically enter Spain for stays of up to 90 days without a visa. Just pack your valid passport (with at least six months validity remaining), proof of onward or return travel, and get ready to embrace the Gran Canaria sunshine.

Double-Checking Before Takeoff: Essential Documents

Here's a quick checklist to ensure a smooth arrival:

- **Valid Passport:** This is your golden ticket to Gran Canaria. Ensure it has at least six months of validity remaining from your planned date of entry.
- **Proof of Onward or Return Travel:** Spanish immigration officials might ask to see a confirmed flight ticket or other documentation proving you'll be leaving the country within 90 days.
- **Health Insurance:** While not mandatory for entry, having valid health insurance for your trip is highly recommended. It provides peace of mind in case of any unexpected medical situations.

A Gentle Reminder: Double-Check Your Nationality's Requirements

While most nationalities enjoy visa-free entry, it's always best to double-check the specific requirements for your country. The Spanish Ministry of Foreign Affairs website (https://www.exteriores.gob.es/) provides a comprehensive list with up-to-date information. This ensures there are no surprises at the airport and allows you to breeze through immigration with confidence.

Beyond the Basics: Considerations for Longer Stays or Special Circumstances

If you're planning a stay exceeding 90 days, pursuing studies in Gran Canaria, or intend to work there, the visa requirements become more nuanced. In such cases, you'll need to apply for the appropriate visa type at the nearest Spanish embassy or consulate well in advance of your trip. Their websites can provide detailed information on the application process and required documents.

Traveling with a Minor? Additional Documents Might Be Required

If you're traveling with children under 18, it's important to be aware of any specific requirements. In some cases, if a minor is traveling with only one parent or guardian, a notarized letter of consent from the other parent may be required. Always check the official Spanish government website or consult the nearest Spanish embassy or consulate for the latest regulations regarding traveling with minors.

With a little preparation, navigating Gran Canaria's entry requirements is a breeze. So, go ahead, dust off your swimsuit, pack your sense of adventure, and get ready to experience the magic of this captivating island!

Packing Essentials

let's talk about packing. Imagine this: you arrive at the airport, check in a breeze, and then...dread. You forgot your swimsuit! Or worse, you packed a bulky winter coat for an island known for its year-round sunshine. Fear not, fellow traveler! This chapter is your personal packing guru, ensuring you arrive prepared and ready to conquer Gran Canaria in style.

Sun Seekers Rejoice: Beach Essentials

The Canary Islands are synonymous with stunning beaches. Pack a minimum of two swimsuits - one for splashing around and another for drying off quickly. Opt for quick-drying materials that won't leave you feeling damp throughout the day. Don't forget a lightweight cover-up for those post-swim strolls along the beach promenade.

Sun protection is paramount. Pack a wide-brimmed hat and sunglasses that offer UV protection. Sunscreen, of course, is essential. Choose a reef-safe, broad-spectrum SPF 30 or higher for adequate protection. Your skin will thank you later!

Beach days are synonymous with relaxation. Pack a lightweight beach towel that dries quickly and takes up minimal space in your luggage. Throw in a good book for those quiet moments under the Canarian sun or a waterproof pouch for your phone if you plan on capturing underwater adventures.

Island Adventures: Clothing for Every Occasion

While you'll spend a good portion of your time basking on the beach, Gran Canaria offers much more. Hiking trails weave through volcanic landscapes, charming towns beckon exploration, and evenings might involve a touch of elegance. Here's what to pack for versatility:

- **Comfortable Walking Shoes:** Pack a sturdy pair of walking shoes or sandals with good tread for exploring the island's diverse terrain. Opt for breathable materials to keep your feet cool and comfortable.
- **Light and Breezy Clothing:** Pack plenty of lightweight, breathable clothing like cotton t-shirts, shorts, and sundresses. Consider quick-drying fabrics for those days filled with adventure.
- **Long Pants and a Light Jacket:** Even in paradise, evenings can get a little cooler, especially in higher altitudes. Pack a pair of long pants and a light jacket for added comfort.
- **Dressy Option (Optional):** If you plan on indulging in a fancy dinner or exploring the nightlife in Las Palmas, pack one dressier outfit. A versatile dress or a pair of slacks with a nice top will suffice.

Essentials No Traveler Should Forget:

Now, let's talk about those travel essentials that make all the difference:

- **Toiletries:** Pack the basics like shampoo, conditioner, soap, and toothpaste. Consider travel-sized versions to save space, especially if you're packing light.
- **Sunscreen and Aftersun Lotion:** As mentioned before, sun protection is crucial. Pack a good quality sunscreen and a soothing aftersun lotion to keep your skin healthy and happy.
- **First-Aid Kit:** Pack a small first-aid kit with essential supplies like bandages, antiseptic wipes, and pain relievers for any minor cuts, scrapes, or headaches.
- **Universal Adapter:** If you're traveling from outside Europe, pack a universal adapter to ensure you can charge your electronic devices.
- **Reusable Water Bottle:** Stay hydrated throughout your trip with a reusable water bottle. It's eco-friendly and saves you money on buying bottled water every day.

Bonus Tip: Pack a quick-drying laundry bag. This allows you to easily wash a few light items during your trip, saving you space in your luggage and the need to pack too many clothes.

Remember, packing light is key! Gran Canaria is a beautiful island that begs to be explored. By packing smart and following these tips, you'll be ready to hit the ground running and create unforgettable memories in this Canarian paradise.

Trip Planning Tools and Resources

Now comes the exciting (and sometimes overwhelming) part: planning your itinerary. Fear not, intrepid traveler! This chapter is your one-stop shop for all the trip planning tools and resources you'll need to craft the perfect Gran Canaria escape.

Imagine yourself lounging on a secluded beach, the volcanic peaks of the island dominating the horizon. Or picture yourself exploring the bustling streets of Las Palmas, vibrant architecture lining your path. To turn these dreams into reality, let's delve into the treasure trove of resources at your disposal.

Websites:

- **Official Gran Canaria Tourism Board:** This website (https://www.grancanaria.com/turismo/) is your official guide to the island. Packed with information on everything from attractions and beaches to events and accommodation, it's a fantastic starting point. Bookmark it - you'll be referring to it often!
- **Travel Blogs:** Get inspired by fellow adventurers who have already explored Gran Canaria. Search for travel blogs that specialize in the Canary Islands or focus on specific travel styles (hiking, budget travel, family travel) to discover hidden gems and unique experiences.

Apps:

- **Google Maps:** This essential app will be your digital Gran Canaria companion. Download offline maps before your trip so you can navigate with

ease, even without an internet connection. Mark all the must-see sights and restaurants you discover during your research to create a personalized map for your adventures.
- **TripAdvisor:** Leverage the collective wisdom of travelers! Use TripAdvisor to research attractions, read reviews on restaurants and hotels, and discover hidden gems recommended by other explorers.

Guidebooks:

While the internet offers a wealth of information, there's something special about holding a physical guidebook. Consider these options:

- **DK Eyewitness Travel Guide: Top 10 Gran Canaria:** This pocket-sized guide is perfect for travelers on the go. It highlights the top 10 attractions and offers handy itineraries for maximizing your time.
- **The Mini Rough Guide to Gran Canaria:** This comprehensive guide dives deeper into the island's culture, history, and hidden corners. It provides recommendations for different travel styles and includes helpful maps.

Pro Tip: Don't just rely on one source. Combine information from websites, travel blogs, guidebooks, and apps to create a well-rounded picture of Gran Canaria and tailor your itinerary to your specific interests and travel style.

Planning Your Itinerary:

Now that you're armed with resources, let's get down to brass tacks - crafting your itinerary! Here are some insider tips to streamline the process:

1. **Consider Your Travel Style:** Are you an adventure seeker who thrives on adrenaline-pumping activities? Or do you prefer to relax on pristine beaches and soak up the sun? Identifying your travel style will help you prioritize the experiences you want to include.
2. **Research Must-See Sights:** Every traveler has their "bucket list" attractions. Whether it's scaling the majestic Pico de las Nieves or

exploring the charming village of Tejeda, make a list of the places you absolutely don't want to miss.
3. **Factor in Travel Time:** Don't underestimate travel time between locations, especially if you plan on exploring different regions of the island. Utilize Google Maps to estimate travel times between attractions to avoid cramming too much into one day.
4. **Leave Room for Spontaneity:** While planning is essential, leave some room for flexibility. You may stumble upon a charming local festival or discover a hidden beach that wasn't on your radar. Embrace the unexpected – it's often during these spontaneous moments that the most memorable travel experiences unfold.

Remember: Planning your Gran Canaria trip should be an enjoyable process. So grab a cup of coffee, browse the resources, and start dreaming! Before you know it, you'll be strolling along Gran Canaria's volcanic shores, with memories waiting to be made.

Where to Stay in Gran Canaria

Finding the perfect place to lay your head after a day of exploring Gran Canaria's vibrant culture and stunning landscapes is crucial. Imagine this: you sink into a plush armchair on your balcony, a cool drink in hand, as the golden sun dips below the horizon, painting the sky in fiery hues. This blissful scene can be your reality, depending on where you choose to stay on this captivating island.

Gran Canaria caters to a variety of travel styles and budgets, offering an array of accommodation options across distinct regions. Let's delve into the unique charm of each area and explore the types of stays that await you:

The Bustling South: Beach Resorts and Family Fun

The southern shores of Gran Canaria are synonymous with sunshine, golden sands, and lively resorts. Here, you'll find a plethora of all-inclusive hotels and family-friendly resorts, perfect for those seeking a hassle-free vacation. Popular areas like Playa del Inglés, Puerto Rico, and Maspalomas boast a vibrant atmosphere with an abundance of restaurants, bars, and shops right at your doorstep.

Pros:

- Direct access to stunning beaches
- Wide variety of hotels, resorts, and apartments
- Family-friendly amenities like pools, kids' clubs, and watersports rentals
- Lively nightlife scene with bars and restaurants

Cons:

- Can be quite crowded, especially during peak season
- Prices tend to be higher compared to other regions
- May not be ideal for those seeking a quieter, more authentic experience

Finding the perfect family-friendly resort in Gran Canaria's sunny south is easy with so many fantastic options. Here are a few suggestions to get you started, each offering something unique for your unforgettable beach vacation:

Hotel: Sunwing Sandy Beach Resort

Address: Av. Estados Unidos, 1, 35100 Maspalomas, Spain
Contact: +34 928 56 00 00
Website: https://www.tripadvisor.com/Hotel_Review-g262055-d1018665-Reviews-Sunwing_Sandy_Bay_Beach-Ayia_Napa_Famagusta_District.html
Average Nightly Rate: €150 - €250
Amenities: This all-inclusive resort is a haven for families. Splash around in the multiple pools, including a dedicated children's pool with slides. The kids' club keeps little ones entertained with daily activities and games, while parents can relax by the pool with a refreshing cocktail. In the evenings, enjoy vibrant family-friendly shows and themed buffets catering to all tastes.

Star Rating: 4-star
Check-In/Out Times: Check-in: 3:00 PM, Check-out: 12:00 PM

Hotel: Gloria Palace Royal Hotel & Spa

Address: Av. Oasis Meloneras, 22, 35100 Meloneras, Spain
Contact: +34 928 73 03 00
Website: https://www.gloriapalaceth.com/en/gloria-palace-royal-hotel-and-spa/
Average Nightly Rate: €200 - €300
Amenities: This luxurious resort offers something for everyone. Relax on the stunning beachfront, take a dip in the lagoon-style pool, or treat yourself to a pampering session at the on-site spa. Kids will love the waterpark with slides and splash areas, while teens can enjoy the games room and organized activities. Spacious rooms with balconies overlooking the pool or ocean make for a comfortable and relaxing family vacation.
Star Rating: 5-star
Check-In/Out Times: Check-in: 3:00 PM, Check-out: 12:00 PM

Apartments: Vista Oasis Meloneras

Address: Calle Las Dunas, 4, 35100 Meloneras, Spain
Contact: +34 928 73 41 14
Website: [Find a listing website for Vista Oasis Meloneras apartments] **(Note:** this may require searching a vacation rental website)
Average Nightly Rate: €100 - €150
Amenities: Opt for a more homey feel with a stay at Vista Oasis Meloneras. These beautifully appointed apartments offer a spacious living area, fully equipped kitchens, and private balconies overlooking the pool or gardens. Perfect for families who crave a bit more independence, you can cook meals in the apartment or venture out to nearby restaurants. The complex boasts a

swimming pool and a children's pool, ideal for cooling off after a day at the beach.
Star Rating: Self-catering Apartment

Hotel: Lopesan Baobab Resort

Address: Av. Cristóbal García Morales, 1, 35100 Maspalomas, Spain**
Contact: +34 928 72 59 00
Website: https://www.lopesan.com/en/hotels/spain/gran-canaria/meloneras/baobab-resort/
Average Nightly Rate: €250 - €350
Amenities: Immerse your family in an African safari experience at the unique Lopesan Baobab Resort. This whimsical resort boasts a giant baobab tree centerpiece, cascading waterfalls, and swim-up bars for a truly memorable stay. The kids' club offers themed activities based on African wildlife, while the numerous pools and water slides provide endless entertainment.
Star Rating: 5-star
Check-In/Out Times: Check-in: 3:00 PM, Check-out: 12:00 PM

Hotel: Riu Gran Canaria

Address: Av. Oasis Meloneras, 7, 35100 Meloneras, Spain**
Contact: +34 928 73 00 00
Website: https://www.riu.com/en/hotel/spain/gran-canaria/clubhotel-riu-gran-canaria/
Average Nightly Rate: €180 - €280
Amenities: This all-inclusive resort is a perfect choice for families seeking a vibrant and action-packed vacation. The large pool complex with water slides and a lazy river will keep kids entertained for hours. Adults can enjoy a variety of sports activities or relax by the pool with a drink in hand. The on-site restaurants cater to all tastes, from international buffets to themed dinners.

Nightly entertainment with live music and shows ensures there's something for everyone to enjoy after a fun-filled day.
Star Rating: 4-star
Check-In/Out Times: Check-in: 3:00 PM, Check-out: 12:00 PM

Bungalows: Anfi Del Mar

Address: Calle Anfi del Mar, 35120 Mogán, Spain**
Contact: +34 928 56 00 00
Website: https://www.anfi.com/
Average Nightly Rate: €120 - €200
Amenities: Nestled amidst lush gardens, Anfi Del Mar offers charming bungalows perfect for families. Choose from one or two-bedroom options, each with a private terrace and a kitchenette. The complex boasts multiple swimming pools, a children's playground, and a variety of on-site restaurants and bars. Relax on the beautiful beach, a short walk away, or participate in water sports activities like kayaking and windsurfing.
Star Rating: Self-catering Bungalows

Hotel: Seaside Sandy Beach

Address: Av. Estados Unidos, 14, 35100 Maspalomas, Spain**
Contact: +34 928 73 03 50
Website: https://www.hotel-sandy-beach.com
Average Nightly Rate: €130 - €220
Amenities: This family-friendly resort offers a relaxed beachfront location close to the lively resort center. Splash around in the large pool with a dedicated children's section, or unwind on the sun loungers by the poolside. The kids' club keeps little ones entertained with daily activities, while parents can enjoy a game of tennis or a massage at the spa. Spacious rooms with balconies ensure a comfortable stay, and the on-site restaurants offer a variety of international cuisines.
Star Rating: 4-star

Check-In/Out Times: Check-in: 3:00 PM, Check-out: 12:00 PM

Apartments: Vista Bonita

Address: Calle Mar Caribe, 1, 35100 Playa del Inglés, Spain**
Contact: +34 928 73 00 00
Website: [Find a listing website for Vista Bonita apartments] **(Note:** this may require searching a vacation rental website)
Average Nightly Rate: €80 - €120
Amenities: For a budget-friendly option, consider Vista Bonita Apartments in Playa del Inglés. These conveniently located apartments offer a comfortable living space with a kitchenette and a balcony. The complex boasts a swimming pool and a children's pool, perfect for a refreshing dip after a day at the beach. Just steps away from restaurants, shops, and the lively resort center, these apartments offer a great base for exploring the bustling south.
Star Rating: Self-catering Apartment

Insider Tip: If you're a family with young children, consider staying near a resort with a dedicated kids' club and splash park. This allows parents to enjoy some well-deserved relaxation while the little ones are entertained.

The Chic North: Boutique Hotels and Ocean Views

The northern shores offer a more laid-back and sophisticated atmosphere. Picturesque towns like Mogán, Amadores, and Puerto de las Nieves boast charming boutique hotels, luxury villas, and self-catering apartments with breathtaking ocean views. Imagine waking up to the gentle sound of waves lapping against the shore and enjoying your morning coffee on a private terrace overlooking the turquoise waters. Absolute bliss!

Pros:

- Stunning ocean views and a more relaxed atmosphere

- Upscale accommodation options with unique architecture and personalized service
- Ideal for couples and travelers seeking a touch of luxury
- Close proximity to charming towns and local restaurants

Cons:

- Limited all-inclusive options
- Fewer shops and restaurants compared to the south
- May require renting a car for easier exploration

The north of Gran Canaria offers a different kind of magic. Here, charming towns and boutique hotels nestled in volcanic landscapes provide a haven for relaxation and stunning ocean vistas. Let's explore some unique options to inspire your chic northern escape:

Hotel: Salobre Resort Serenity

Address: Barranco de Salobre Golf, s/n, 35100 Maspalomas, Spain**
Contact: +34 928 56 80 00
Average Nightly Rate: €180 - €300
Amenities: Nestled amidst a championship golf course, Salobre Resort Serenity offers a tranquil escape with stunning mountain and ocean views. Relax by the infinity pool overlooking the dramatic landscape, indulge in a rejuvenating treatment at the on-site spa, or explore the nearby charming villages.
Star Rating: 5-star
Check-In/Out Times: Check-in: 3:00 PM, Check-out: 12:00 PM

Boutique Hotel: Las Gaviotas Suites

Address: Calle Las Gaviotas, 2, 35450 Mogán, Spain**
Contact: +34 928 56 00 51
Website: https://www.hotellasgaviotas.com/
Average Nightly Rate: €150 - €250

Amenities: This intimate boutique hotel oozes Canarian charm. Located in the heart of Mogán's harbor town, you'll be steps away from charming cafes, fresh seafood restaurants, and lively markets. Wake up to stunning views of the marina from your private balcony and spend your days exploring the town's cobbled streets or lounging by the rooftop pool.
Star Rating: 4-star
Check-In/Out Times: Check-in: 2:00 PM, Check-out: 11:00 AM

Apartments: Amadores Beach Apartments

Address: Calle del Mar, 10, 35450 Amadores, Spain**
Contact: [Find a listing website for Amadores Beach Apartments] (**Note:** this may require searching a vacation rental website)
Average Nightly Rate: €100 - €150
Amenities: For a more independent experience, consider Amadores Beach Apartments. These modern apartments offer stunning ocean views, fully equipped kitchens, and private balconies. Perfect for families or groups of friends, you can enjoy the flexibility of preparing meals or venturing out to explore the local culinary scene. Relax on the complex's sun terrace or stroll down to the beautiful Amadores Beach, just steps away.
Star Rating: Self-catering Apartment

Hotel: The Cliff Bay Hotel

Address: Carretera Arucas a Mogán, Km. 12, 35450 Mogán, Spain**
Contact: +34 928 56 02 72
Average Nightly Rate: €200 - €350
Amenities: Perched on a cliff overlooking the ocean, The Cliff Bay Hotel offers a truly breathtaking setting. Spacious rooms with private balconies provide stunning panoramic views, while the infinity pool seems to melt into the ocean horizon. Indulge in delicious meals at the hotel's gourmet restaurant with ocean views, or take a dip in the jacuzzi while gazing at the star-studded sky. This hotel is perfect for a romantic getaway or a luxurious escape for discerning travelers.

Star Rating: 5-star
Check-In/Out Times: Check-in: 3:00 PM, Check-out: 12:00 PM

Boutique Hotel: Casa del Mar

Address: Calle Drago, 8, 35460 Puerto de las Nieves, Spain**
Contact: +34 928 80 59 00
Average Nightly Rate: €120 - €200
Amenities: Step back in time at the charming Casa del Mar. This beautifully restored 18th-century Canarian house offers a unique and intimate stay. The rooftop terrace boasts stunning ocean views, perfect for enjoying a leisurely breakfast or an evening glass of wine. Explore the nearby fishing village of Puerto de las Nieves, known for its colorful houses and laid-back atmosphere.
Star Rating: 4-star
Check-In/Out Times: Check-in: 2:00 PM, Check-out: 11:00 AM

Eco-Finca La yurta

Address: Barranco de Guayadeque, s/n, 35119 Artenara, Spain**
Contact: +34 622 68 45 42
Average Nightly Rate: €100 - €180
Amenities: For a truly unique experience, immerse yourself in nature at Eco-Finca La Yurta. Stay in a luxurious yurt nestled amidst a dramatic volcanic landscape. The yurts feature comfortable beds, private bathrooms, and furnished patios offering stunning mountain views. Enjoy hikes in the surrounding area, unwind in the natural swimming pool, or stargaze under the clear night sky.
Star Rating: Glamping

Hotel: Barceló Arguineguín Resort

Address: Calle Lomo Quiebre, 1, 35120 Arguineguín, Spain**

Contact: +34 928 15 00 00
Average Nightly Rate: €130 - €220
Amenities: This modern resort offers stunning ocean views and a variety of amenities for a relaxing stay. Spacious rooms with balconies overlook the sparkling pool complex and the ocean beyond. Enjoy delicious meals at the on-site restaurants, participate in water sports activities on the beach, or simply relax by the pool and soak up the sunshine.
Star Rating: 4-star
Check-In/Out Times: Check-in: 3:00 PM, Check-out: 12:00 PM

Insider Tip: If you're a couple seeking a romantic getaway, look for a boutique hotel with a rooftop terrace or an infinity pool with stunning ocean views. The perfect setting for creating unforgettable memories.

Las Palmas: Urban Vibes and Cultural Immersion

The vibrant city of Las Palmas offers a unique accommodation experience. Stay in the heart of the action, close to historical landmarks, museums, and bustling markets. A variety of hotels, stylish apartments, and charming guesthouses cater to different tastes and budgets. Imagine strolling cobbled streets lined with colorful architecture, popping into local cafes for tapas, and enjoying the buzzing nightlife scene. Las Palmas offers a truly immersive cultural experience.

Pros:

- Close proximity to cultural attractions, museums, and historical sites
- Lively atmosphere with a variety of restaurants, bars, and shops
- Wide range of accommodation options to suit all budgets
- Excellent public transportation network for exploring the city

Cons:

- Limited direct beach access (beaches are a short bus ride away)
- Can be quite noisy, especially in the city center

Las Palmas offers a unique blend of urban energy, cultural immersion, and beautiful beaches. Here are some accommodation options to suit different tastes, all within easy reach of the city's vibrant core:

Hotel: Santa Catalina, a Royal Hideaway Hotel

Address: Plaza de Santa Catalina, s/n, 35001 Las Palmas de Gran Canaria, Spain** **Contact:** +34 928 38 14 00
Average Nightly Rate: €300 - €500
Amenities: Steeped in history and elegance, this iconic hotel overlooks the bustling Plaza de Santa Catalina. Imagine sipping your morning coffee on a balcony overlooking the lively square, people-watching as the city comes alive. Spacious rooms with plush furnishings and modern amenities ensure a luxurious stay, while the rooftop pool offers stunning city and ocean views.
Star Rating: 5-star
Check-In/Out Times: Check-in: 3:00 PM, Check-out: 12:00 PM

Hotel: Hotel Acuario Atlántico

Address: Calle Luis Morote, 22, 35001 Las Palmas de Gran Canaria, Spain** **Contact:** +34 928 36 12 00

Average Nightly Rate: €100 - €150
Amenities: This modern hotel is a great choice for budget-conscious travelers seeking a central location. Steps away from Las Canteras Beach and the city's vibrant promenade, you'll be perfectly positioned to explore all that Las Palmas offers. The rooftop terrace boasts panoramic city views and a refreshing pool, perfect for a relaxing afternoon after a day of sightseeing.
Star Rating: 3-star

Check-In/Out Times: Check-in: 2:00 PM, Check-out: 12:00 PM

Boutique Hotel: Hotel Boutique Emblem Las Palmas

Address: Calle Cano 4, 35001 Las Palmas de Gran Canaria, Spain **
Contact: +34 928 36 33 00
Average Nightly Rate: €150 - €200
Amenities: Immerse yourself in Canarian charm at this beautifully restored 18th-century building. Located in the historic Vegueta district, you'll be surrounded by cobbled streets, architectural gems, and charming cafes. The hotel's rooftop terrace provides a tranquil oasis with stunning city views, while the intimate courtyard offers a peaceful escape.
Star Rating: 4-star
Check-In/Out Times: Check-in: 3:00 PM, Check-out: 12:00 PM

Apartments: Las Palmas City Apartments

Address: Various Locations Throughout Las Palmas City Center, Spain **
Contact: [Find a listing website for Las Palmas City Apartments] (**Note:** this may require searching a vacation rental website)
Average Nightly Rate: €75 - €125 **Amenities:** Experience Las Palmas like a local by staying in a vacation rental apartment. This option offers a more independent stay with the flexibility to prepare meals in a fully equipped kitchen. Many apartments boast balconies overlooking bustling streets or charming plazas, allowing you to truly soak up the city's vibrant atmosphere.
Star Rating: Self-catering Apartment

Hotel: NH Las Palmas Playa Cristina

Address: Calle Luis Morote, 41, 35007 Las Palmas de Gran Canaria, Spain **
Contact: +34 928 36 11 00
Average Nightly Rate: €120 - €180
Amenities: This modern hotel is a perfect choice for those seeking

Amenities: This modern hotel is a perfect choice for those seeking a comfortable stay with easy beach access. Located right on the Las Canteras beachfront promenade, you can step out your door and onto the golden sands. The hotel boasts a rooftop pool with stunning ocean views, a perfect spot to relax after a day of swimming and exploring the city.
Star Rating: 4-star
Check-In/Out Times: Check-in: 3:00 PM, Check-out: 12:00 PM

Guest House: Casa Agaete

Address: Calle Cano, 29, 35001 Las Palmas de Gran Canaria, Spain **
Contact: +34 928 36 29 00
Average Nightly Rate: €80 - €120
Amenities: Experience Canarian hospitality at Casa Agaete, a charming guest house housed in a traditional Canarian townhouse. Located in the historic Vegueta district, you'll be surrounded by local life and cultural attractions. The guest house offers comfortable rooms with a shared kitchen and a rooftop terrace, a perfect spot to enjoy a leisurely breakfast with city views.
Star Rating: Guest House

Boutique Hotel: Hotel Las Palmas Urban

Address: Calle Tomás Miller, 32, 35007 Las Palmas de Gran Canaria, Spain **
Contact: +34 928 37 00 00
Average Nightly Rate: €200 - €300
Amenities: This stylish hotel offers a modern take on Canarian charm. Located in the heart of the city's commercial district, you'll be surrounded by shops, restaurants, and cultural attractions. The hotel boasts a rooftop bar with panoramic city views, a perfect spot to sip cocktails and soak up the vibrant atmosphere.
Star Rating: 4-star
Check-In/Out Times: Check-in: 3:00 PM, Check-out: 12:00 PM

Apartments: Vegueta Suites

Address: Calle Pelayo, 11, 35001 Las Palmas de Gran Canaria, Spain **
Contact: [Find a listing website for Vegueta Suites] (**Note:** this may require searching a vacation rental website)
Average Nightly Rate: €100 - €150 **Amenities:** Immerse yourself in the heart of history by staying in a beautifully restored apartment in the Vegueta district. These charming apartments boast traditional Canarian architecture with modern amenities, offering a comfortable and unique stay. Step outside your door and explore cobbled streets lined with historical landmarks, museums, and charming cafes.
Star Rating: Self-catering Apartment

Remember, choosing where to stay in Las Palmas depends on your desired experience. Do you crave a luxurious stay with stunning views, or a charming and historic setting? With this variety of options, you're sure to find the perfect home base for your Las Palmas adventure.

Insider Tip: Book an apartment with a balcony overlooking Plaza de Santa Catalina. This lively square is the heart of the city and offers a vibrant atmosphere perfect for people-watching and enjoying the local culture.

Remember, choosing where to stay is a personal decision. Consider your travel style, budget, and desired experiences. Do you crave a beachfront resort with all the trimmings, or a charming boutique hotel with a local touch?

Part 2: Unveiling Gran Canaria's Treasures

Top Tourist Attractions & Activities

Gran Canaria is a captivating island overflowing with mesmerizing sights, historical gems, awe-inspiring natural wonders, and vibrant cultural experiences. This chapter will be your guide to the island's must-see attractions and unforgettable activities, ensuring your Gran Canaria adventure is packed with memories that last a lifetime.

1. The Enigmatic Roque Nublo

- **Address:** Roque Nublo Rural Park, Artenara, Gran Canaria, Spain
- **Contact:** Gran Canaria Natural Parks Authority: +34 928 35 11 00
- **Website:** https://www.visitcanaryislands.org/gran-canaria-natrual-parks
- **Opening Hours:** Accessible 24/7
- **Closing Hours:** N/A
- **Directions:** Roque Nublo is located in the center of the island. From Las Palmas, take the GC-6 motorway towards Tejeda and Artenara. Follow signs for Roque Nublo and the viewpoint (Mirador de la Degollada de la Cumbre).
- **Activity Cost:** Free to access the Roque Nublo viewpoint and hiking trails.
- **Additional Info:** Wear sturdy shoes for hiking and be prepared for windy conditions at the summit.

Roque Nublo, a majestic volcanic rock formation towering over 1,800 meters above sea level, is a Gran Canaria icon. Enveloped in ancient legends and shrouded in mist, this natural wonder is a must-visit for anyone seeking breathtaking landscapes and a touch of adventure.

Hike the well-maintained trails leading to the Roque Nublo viewpoint and be rewarded with panoramic vistas of the island's dramatic volcanic landscapes.

On a clear day, you can see neighboring islands like Tenerife and Fuerteventura. Imagine standing at the foot of this awe-inspiring rock, feeling a sense of history and marveling at the power of nature.

2. Whale and Dolphin Watching

- **Activity Cost:** Tours typically range from €50 - €100 per person (depending on duration and inclusions)
- **Additional Info:** Whale and dolphin watching tours typically depart from Puerto Mogán, Puerto Rico, and Arguineguín. Choose tours with responsible operators who prioritize animal welfare.

Embark on an unforgettable journey into the Atlantic Ocean in search of majestic whales and playful dolphins. Gran Canaria's waters are home to a diverse marine population, and spotting these incredible creatures in their natural habitat is a truly magical experience.

Imagine the thrill of seeing a pod of dolphins gracefully leaping through the waves or a majestic whale breaching the water's surface. Many tours offer additional perks like snorkeling or swimming in secluded coves, making it a full-day adventure for the whole

3. The Village of Tejeda

- **Address:** Tejeda, Gran Canaria, Spain
- **Contact:** Tejeda Tourist Office: +34 928 66 60 03
- **Website:** N/A (There's no official website, but you can find information through Gran Canaria tourism websites)
- **Opening Hours:** Village is accessible 24/7, shops and restaurants have individual hours.
- **Closing Hours:** Village is accessible 24/7, shops and restaurants have individual hours.
- **Directions:** Tejeda is located in the center of the island. From Las Palmas, take the GC-6 motorway towards Tejeda.
- **Activity Cost:** Free to explore the village.

- **Additional Info:** Tejeda is a car-dependent village with limited public transportation options. Consider renting a car for the ultimate flexibility in exploring the island's interior.

Nestled amidst the island's mountainous heart lies Tejeda, a charming village oozing with Canarian charm. Imagine strolling through cobbled streets lined with whitewashed houses adorned with colorful flowerpots. Time seems to slow down in Tejeda, offering a welcome escape from the hustle and bustle of coastal resorts.

Stop by a local restaurant and savor a traditional Canarian dish like "papas arrugadas" (wrinkled potatoes) with "mojo" sauce, or indulge in a slice of freshly baked almond cake, a local specialty. Visit the 18th-century church, Iglesia de Santa Lucia de Tejeda, and admire its intricate architecture. Tejeda is also known for its surrounding almond groves. If you visit in February, you'll be treated to a breathtaking spectacle as the entire landscape explodes in a blanket of white blossoms.

4. Vulcan Crater Tour

- **Activity Cost:** Tours typically range from €30 - €50 per person (depending on duration and inclusions)
- **Additional Info:** Several companies offer guided hikes and crater tours. Choose tours with experienced guides who can share the fascinating geological history of the island.

Gran Canaria's volcanic origins have sculpted a dramatic landscape, and exploring a volcanic crater is a must-do activity for any nature enthusiast. Several companies offer guided hikes to various craters, each with its unique characteristics.

Imagine descending into the heart of a dormant volcano, marveling at the colorful volcanic rock formations and the sheer scale of these natural wonders. Learn from your guide about the island's volcanic history and the impact it has had on shaping the landscape. Many tours also include visits to volcanic caves, offering a glimpse into the island's hidden underground world.

5. Mercado Central de Las Palmas

- **Address:** Calle Luis Morote, 20, 35001 Las Palmas de Gran Canaria, Spain
- **Opening Hours:** Monday - Saturday: 8:00 AM to 2:00 PM
- **Closing Hours:** Closed on Sundays
- **Directions:** Located in the heart of Las Palmas, a short walk from Santa Catalina Park.
- **Activity Cost:** Free to enter, cost depends on purchases made.
- **Additional Info:** Come hungry! Sample local delicacies, fresh produce, and traditional Canarian products.

Immerse yourself in the vibrant sights, sounds, and aromas of the Mercado Central de Las Palmas, a bustling marketplace showcasing the island's culinary delights. Wander through stalls overflowing with fresh fruits and vegetables in an explosion of colors. Sample exotic local

6. Aqualand Maspalomas

- **Address:** Av. Cristóbal García Morales Km. 2, 35100 Maspalomas, Spain
- **Contact:** +34 928 73 50 00
- **Website:** https://www.aqualand.es/maspalomas/en/
- **Opening Hours:** Varies depending on the season, typically 10:00 AM to 5:00 PM
- **Closing Hours:** Varies depending on the season, typically 5:00 PM
- **Directions:** Located in Maspalomas, south of the island. Accessible by car, taxi, or public bus.
- **Activity Cost:** Entrance fees vary depending on age and season (expect to pay around €30 for adults)
- **Additional Info:** Perfect for families and thrill-seekers. Lockers and sun loungers available for rent.

For a day filled with aquatic fun and adrenaline-pumping rides, head to Aqualand Maspalomas, the island's largest water park. Imagine screaming with delight as you plummet down a colossal water slide or feel the weightlessness of a freefall drop. Relax and unwind in the lazy river or spend quality time with your family in the wave pool. For younger children, there's a dedicated splash park with smaller slides and water features.

Aqualand Maspalomas caters to all ages and thrill levels. Grab a refreshing drink and some snacks from the on-site restaurants and cafes to keep your energy levels up throughout the day. This water park offers a welcome respite from the hot Gran Canarian sun and guarantees a day filled with laughter and unforgettable memories.

7. Guayadeque Ravine

- **Address:** Barranco de Guayadeque, Gran Canaria, Spain
- **Contact:** Gran Canaria Tourist Board: +34 928 30 26 00
- **Website:** https://www.grancanaria.com/turismo/en/10-highlights-not-to-be-missed/ (This website mentions Guayadeque Ravine under "10 Highlights not to be missed")
- **Opening Hours:** Accessible during daylight hours
- **Closing Hours:** N/A
- **Directions:** Located in the center of the island, south of Artenara. Accessible by car following signs for "Barranco de Guayadeque."
- **Activity Cost:** Free to explore, some museums or shops may have entrance fees.
- **Additional Info:** Wear comfortable shoes suitable for walking on uneven terrain. Bring plenty of water, especially on hot days.

Step back in time and explore the Guayadeque Ravine, a fascinating historical and cultural treasure trove. Imagine walking through a dramatic canyon, its walls dotted with ancient dwellings carved into the volcanic rock by the indigenous people, the Guanches. These troglodyte homes, known as "casas cueva" (cave houses), offer a glimpse into the island's pre-Hispanic past.

Several museums within the ravine showcase artifacts and exhibits detailing the lives of the Guanches. You can even visit a reconstructed G

8. Tamadaba National Park

- **Address:** Tamadaba National Park Visitor Center, Agaete, Gran Canaria, Spain
- **Contact:** Tamadaba National Park Visitor Center: +34 928 89 80 03
- **Website:** https://www.holaislascanarias.com/espacios-naturales/gran-canaria/parque-natural-de-tamadaba/ (Spanish only, you can use a translation tool)
- **Opening Hours:** Park accessible during daylight hours, Visitor Center hours may vary.
- **Closing Hours:** Park accessible during daylight hours, Visitor Center hours may vary.
- **Directions:** Located in the northwestern part of the island. Accessible by car or public bus to Agaete, then a taxi or short walk to designated trails.
- **Activity Cost:** Free to enter the park.
- **Additional Info:** Choose a trail suitable for your fitness level. The park offers challenging hikes with breathtaking views and shorter, family-friendly paths. Be sure to pack plenty of water, sunscreen, and a hat.

Lace up your hiking boots and embark on an adventure through Tamadaba National Park, a haven of lush greenery and dramatic landscapes. Imagine trekking through a dense pine forest, breathing in the fresh mountain air and marveling at the vibrant tapestry of flora and fauna. Keep your eyes peeled for endemic bird species and playful rabbits that call this park home.

Tamadaba National Park offers a network of well-maintained trails catering to all experience levels. For seasoned hikers, challenging ascents lead to breathtaking panoramic vistas of the island's northwest coast. Shorter, family-friendly trails meander through valleys and offer a more leisurely way to experience the park's beauty. A visit to Tamadaba National Park is a chance to reconnect with nature and appreciate Gran Canaria's diverse ecosystems.

9. Snorkeling & Diving Tour

- **Activity Cost:** Tours typically range from €50 - €100 per person (depending on duration, location, and equipment rental)
- **Additional Info:** Several companies offer snorkeling and diving tours at various locations around the island. Choose a reputable operator with experienced guides who prioritize safety and marine conservation.

Gran Canaria boasts a vibrant underwater world teeming with colorful fish, playful dolphins, and majestic sea turtles. Embark on a snorkeling or diving tour and immerse yourself in this captivating aquatic realm.

Imagine gliding through crystal-clear waters, surrounded by schools of vibrantly colored fish darting between coral reefs. Experienced divers can explore underwater caves and shipwrecks, remnants of the island's rich maritime history. Snorkeling and diving tours are a fantastic way to explore Gran Canaria from a different perspective and create lasting memories beneath the waves.

10. Food Tour in Las Palmas

- **Activity Cost:** Tours typically range from €70 - €100 per person (depending on duration, inclusions, and number of tastings)
- **Additional Info:** Several companies offer food tours in Las Palmas, focusing on local cuisine, cultural experiences, and hidden gems. Choose a tour that aligns with your dietary preferences and interests.

Las Palmas is a foodie paradise, and what better way to experience the city's vibrant culture than through a delicious food tour? Imagine strolling through bustling markets overflowing with fresh, seasonal produce. Sample local delicacies like "ropa vieja" (shredded beef stew), "gofio" (toasted cornmeal), and the ever-present "papas arrugadas" (wrinkled potatoes) with "mojo" sauce.

Food tours typically involve visits to local restaurants, cafes, and specialty shops. You'll not only savor the flavors but also gain insights into Canarian culinary traditions and cooking techniques from passionate local guides. These tours often include stops at hidden gems like family-run bakeries or artisanal cheese shops, offering a taste of authentic Gran Canaria.

11. Astronomical Observatories

- **Address:** Two main options:
    - Observatorio Roque Nublo: San Mateo, Gran Canaria, Spain
    - Observatorio del Teide: Tenerife, Canary Islands, Spain (Optional - Day Trip)
- **Contact:**
    - Observatorio Roque Nublo: +34 928 66 60 03 (Note: Limited public tours offered, booking well in advance is essential)
    - Observatorio del Teide: +34 922 31 54 40 (https://www.iac.es/en/observatorios-de-canarias/teide-observatory)
- **Website:**
    - Observatorio Roque Nublo: N/A (Limited public information available)
    - Observatorio del Teide: https://www.iac.es/en/observatorios-de-canarias/teide-observatory
- **Opening Hours:** Varies depending on the observatory and chosen program. Nighttime observations are typical.
- **Closing Hours:** Varies depending on the observatory and chosen program. Nighttime observations are typical.
- **Directions:**
    - Observatorio Roque Nublo: Located in the center of the island, accessible by car following signs for "Roque Nublo."
    - Observatorio del Teide: Located on the island of Tenerife, a ferry ride away from Gran Canaria. Day trip options are available.
- **Activity Cost:** Varies depending on the observatory and chosen program (expect to pay around €30 - €50 per person).
- **Additional Info:** Dress warmly for nighttime observations at high altitudes. Booking in advance is essential, especially for Roque Nublo tours.

For astronomy enthusiasts or anyone seeking a truly magical experience, a visit to one of Gran Canaria's astronomical observatories is a must. Imagine gazing through powerful telescopes and marveling at the Milky Way galaxy in all its glory, a million miles away from the city lights.

The Observatorio Roque Nublo, perched atop the iconic Roque Nublo rock formation, offers occasional public stargazing nights. However, booking well in advance is crucial due to limited availability. Another option is the renowned Observatorio del Teide on the neighboring island of Tenerife. Day trip tours from Gran Canaria allow you to experience the awe-inspiring telescopes and witness the night sky at this world-class observatory. A visit to an astronomical observatory is a chance to connect with the universe, learn about the wonders of space, and create memories that will stay with you forever.

Las Palmas: Unveiling the vibrant capital city

Las Palmas, the bustling capital of Gran Canaria, pulsates with energy. It's a city that seamlessly blends its rich history and cultural heritage with modern vibrancy. Imagine strolling along the scenic promenade, savoring fresh seafood at a harborside restaurant, or getting lost in the charming cobbled streets of the Vegueta district. Las Palmas offers something for every kind of traveler, from beach lovers and history buffs to art enthusiasts and culture seekers. Let's dive into the heart of this captivating city and explore its hidden gems.

1. Las Canteras Beach

- **Address:** Playa de Las Canteras, Las Palmas de Gran Canaria, Spain
- **Contact:** Las Palmas de Gran Canaria Tourist Board: +34 928 30 26 00
- **Opening Hours:** Accessible 24/7
- **Directions:** Located along the northern coast of Las Palmas. Easily accessible by foot from most city center locations or by bus.
- **Activity Cost:** Free to access the beach. Sun loungers and umbrellas can be rented for a fee.

- **Additional Info:** Las Canteras offers something for everyone - sunbathing, swimming, surfing, bodyboarding, and stand-up paddleboarding. Lifeguards are on duty during peak season.

No trip to Las Palmas would be complete without spending a day basking in the glorious sunshine on the iconic Las Canteras Beach. Imagine stretching out on the golden sand, feeling the warmth of the sun on your skin and the gentle caress of the ocean breeze. This 3-kilometer stretch of pristine coastline is a haven for relaxation and a playground for water sports enthusiasts.

Take a refreshing dip in the crystal-clear waters, perfect for a swim or a leisurely float. For the more adventurous, waves crash along the shore, creating ideal conditions for surfing, bodyboarding, or stand-up paddleboarding. Beach vendors offer refreshing drinks and light snacks, while numerous restaurants and cafes line the beachfront promenade, beckoning you to indulge in a delicious seafood feast after a day spent soaking up the sun.

2. Vegueta Historic Quarter

- **Address:** Vegueta District, Las Palmas de Gran Canaria, Spain
- **Contact:** Las Palmas de Gran Canaria Tourist Board: +34 928 30 26 00
- **Opening Hours:** Individual attractions within Vegueta will have specific opening hours.
- **Closing Hours:** Individual attractions within Vegueta will have specific closing hours.
- **Directions:** Located in the heart of Las Palmas. Easily accessible by foot from most city center locations.
- **Activity Cost:** Free to explore the district, entrance fees may apply for museums and historical sites.
- **Additional Info:** Wear comfortable shoes for walking on cobbled streets. Consider purchasing a Las Palmas City Card for discounted entry to museums and free public transportation.

Step back in time and wander through the charming cobbled streets of Vegueta, Las Palmas' historic heart. Imagine yourself transported to a bygone era, surrounded by colorful colonial buildings adorned with intricate balconies and wrought-iron railings. Each corner reveals a hidden treasure, from the iconic Santa Ana Cathedral, the oldest church in the Canary Islands, to Casa de Colón, believed to be the house of Christopher Columbus on his voyage to the Americas.

Don't miss Plaza de Santa Ana, a lively square buzzing with street performers, bustling cafes, and a vibrant atmosphere. Immerse yourself in Canarian culture by browsing local shops selling handcrafted souvenirs and sampling traditional delicacies at the bustling market. Vegueta is a visual feast, offering a glimpse into Las Palmas' rich past and a delightful escape from the modern world.

3. Museums and Art Galleries

- **Museum & Gallery Locations:** Scattered throughout Las Palmas City Center (addresses below)
- **Contact:** Las Palmas de Gran Canaria Tourist Board: +34 928 30 26 00 (الكناري جزر في لسياحة) (Website in Spanish and English) can help you find specific museums)
- **Website:** Individual museum websites (See below for some suggestions)
- **Opening Hours:** Individual museums will have specific opening hours.
- **Closing Hours:** Individual museums will have specific closing hours. Most museums are closed on Mondays.
- **Directions:** Varies depending on the chosen museum. Many are located within walking distance from each other in the Vegueta district or Las Palmas city center. Public transportation or taxis are readily available for museums further afield.
- **Activity Cost:** Entrance fees vary depending on the museum, with some offering free admission or discounts with a Las Palmas City Card.
- **Additional Info:** Plan your museum visits in advance and check opening hours to avoid disappointment. Consider purchasing a Las Palmas City Card for discounted entry to many museums.

Las Palmas is a treasure trove for art and history enthusiasts. The city boasts a diverse array of museums and art galleries, each offering a unique perspective on the island's culture and heritage. Here are a few highlights to consider:

- **Museo Canario:** Delve into the fascinating history and indigenous culture of Gran Canaria through interactive exhibits and archaeological artifacts.
- **CAAM - Atlantic Center of Modern Art:** Explore contemporary art from the Canary Islands, Africa, and Latin America in this stunning modern building.
- **Casa de Colón:** Step into the house believed to have hosted Christopher Columbus on his voyage to the Americas, and learn about his historic journey.
- **Elder Museum of Science and Technology:** Spark your curiosity with interactive exhibits on science, technology, and astronomy, perfect for families with children.
- **Museo Diocesano de Arte Sacro:** Admire a collection of religious art and artifacts spanning centuries, housed in a beautiful 18th-century building.

This is just a taste of the museums Las Palmas has to offer. Exploring these cultural institutions will enhance your understanding of the island's rich tapestry and provide a deeper appreciation for its artistic heritage.

4. Fiestas and Local Traditions

- **Contact:** Las Palmas de Gran Canaria Tourist Board: +34 928 30 26 00 (الكناري جزر في لسياحة) (Website in Spanish and English) can help you find specific event information.
- **Activity Cost:** Varies depending on the event. Some events are free, while others may have entrance fees.
- **Additional Info:** Plan your trip to coincide with a local festival for a truly immersive experience.

Las Palmas vibrates with life throughout the year, thanks to its vibrant festivals and local traditions. Immerse yourself in the city's infectious energy by attending one of its many fiestas.

- **Carnaval:** Held before Lent, Las Palmas explodes in a kaleidoscope of colors, costumes, and music during its renowned Carnival celebration. Witness elaborate parades, dance the night away at lively street parties, and be swept away by the infectious energy of this joyous event.
- **Fiesta del Carmen:** Held in July, this festival honors the Virgin of Carmen, patron saint of fishermen. Witness a colorful procession of decorated fishing boats and enjoy lively celebrations along the Las Canteras beachfront.
- **Romería de San Benito Abad:** Held in the historic town of San Mateo in October, this traditional pilgrimage features a vibrant procession with colorful costumes, traditional music, and a festive atmosphere.

These are just a few examples of the many festivals and celebrations that bring Las Palmas to life. By participating in these events, you'll gain a deeper understanding of the city's rich culture and traditions, and create memories that will last a lifetime.

Las Palmas offers an unforgettable blend of urban excitement, historical charm, and vibrant culture. Whether you're seeking sun-drenched beaches, fascinating museums, or lively festivals, this captivating city has something for everyone. So, pack your bags, embrace the Las Palmas spirit, and get ready to discover the heart and soul of Gran Canaria.

5. Las Palmas' Gastronomic Delights

Las Palmas is a paradise for foodies, offering a delectable fusion of Canarian and Spanish cuisine with fresh, locally-sourced ingredients. Imagine strolling through bustling market stalls overflowing with exotic fruits, vibrant vegetables, and freshly caught seafood. Indulge in a tapas crawl through charming bars, sampling an array of small plates bursting with flavor. Or, settle into a harborside restaurant and savor a leisurely meal with breathtaking ocean views.

Must-Try Dishes:

- **Papas Arrugadas:** Wrinkled potatoes, a Canarian staple, simply boiled in salted water and served with mojo sauces (red or green).
- **Gofio:** A toasted cornmeal flour used in various dishes, from savory stews to sweet desserts.
- **Ropa Vieja:** A slow-cooked chickpea and meat stew, a comforting and flavorful dish.
- **Queso Asado:** Grilled Canarian cheese, often served with mojo sauces and perfect for sharing.
- **Fresh Seafood:** Sample the daily catch – from succulent prawns and gambas (shrimp) to local fish like cherne (wreckfish) and vieja (parrotfish).

Where to Eat:

- **Vegueta District:** Quaint cafes and traditional tapas bars line the charming streets, perfect for a casual bite or a leisurely lunch.
- **Playa de Las Canteras:** Beachfront restaurants with stunning ocean views offer fresh seafood dishes and a relaxed atmosphere.
- **Mercado Central de Las Palmas:** Immerse yourself in the sights, sounds, and aromas of this bustling market, where you can sample local delicacies or grab fresh ingredients for a picnic.

6. Day Trips from Las Palmas

Las Palmas is a fantastic base for exploring the diverse landscapes and charming towns of Gran Canaria. Rent a car for a day trip adventure and discover hidden gems waiting to be unveiled.

A. **Arucas:**

Just a short drive west of Las Palmas lies Arucas, a charming town aptly nicknamed "The City of Flowers." Imagine strolling along vibrant streets lined with houses adorned with overflowing flower displays in a delightful explosion of color. Arucas isn't just a feast for the eyes; it's also steeped in rich history.

- **Explore the Historical Center:** Wander through the charming pedestrianized streets and admire the colonial architecture, including the iconic red-tiled roofs and traditional Canarian balconies. Don't miss the Iglesia de San Juan Bautista, a beautiful 18th-century church showcasing intricate Baroque details.
- **A Step Back in Time: The Municipal Museum of Arucas** Delve into the town's fascinating past at the Municipal Museum of Arucas. Exhibits showcase the history of Arucas, from its indigenous Guanche heritage to its rise as a rum-producing center.
- **A Sweet Indulgence: Arucas Rum Distillery** No visit to Arucas is complete without experiencing the world-famous Arehucas Rum Distillery. Embark on a guided tour, learn about the traditional rum-making process, and indulge in a tasting of their award-winning rums. The distillery shop offers a variety of rums to purchase as a unique souvenir.

B. **Teror:**

Nestled amidst the lush mountains of Gran Canaria, discover Teror, a picturesque town known for its religious significance and breathtaking scenery.

- **Basilica del Pino: A Pilgrimage Site** The crown jewel of Teror is the magnificent Basilica del Pino, a significant pilgrimage site dedicated to the Virgin of the Pine. Marvel at the neoclassical architecture, ornate interiors, and the venerated statue of the Virgin Mary, believed to be miraculous. Witness the vibrant annual pilgrimage held in September, a colorful celebration attracting thousands of devotees.
- **A Town Adorned with Flowers:** Teror lives up to its reputation as a floral paradise. Imagine strolling through charming streets lined with houses adorned with overflowing flower displays cascading from traditional wooden balconies. The vibrant colors and sweet fragrance create a truly magical atmosphere.
- **Explore the Mountains:** Teror is a fantastic base for exploring the surrounding mountains. Lace up your boots and embark on scenic hikes

through pine forests, offering breathtaking panoramic views and a chance to connect with nature.

C. Bandama Caldera:

Venture into the heart of Gran Canaria's volcanic past at the Bandama Caldera, a dramatic landscape formed by a collapsed volcanic crater. Imagine standing at the rim of this colossal natural wonder, gazing down at the vast caldera floor and the verdant vegetation that has taken root within.

- **A Scenic Hike:** Embark on a moderate hike that leads to the caldera rim. The well-maintained trail offers stunning views of the surrounding landscapes, including volcanic peaks, valleys, and the distant ocean. Keep an eye out for interesting volcanic rock formations and diverse plant life along the way.
- **A Geological Marvel:** Learn about the fascinating geological history of the Bandama Caldera. This natural wonder was formed millions of years ago by a series of volcanic eruptions. Informative panels along the trail offer insights into the volcanic processes that shaped the island.
- **Wine Tasting with a View:** After your hike, consider visiting the nearby Villa Bandama Golf Resort. Enjoy a delicious meal or a glass of locally produced Canarian wine while soaking up the breathtaking panorama of the Bandama Caldera.

D. Puerto de Mogán: A Tranquil Escape on the Coast

Trade the bustling city life for the laid-back charm of Puerto de Mogán, a picturesque fishing village located on Gran Canaria's southwest coast. Imagine strolling along the harbor, admiring colorful fishing boats bobbing on the turquoise waters, and soaking up the relaxed atmosphere.

- **A Picturesque Harbor:** The heart of Puerto de Mogán is its charming harbor. Lined with quaint cafes and restaurants with outdoor terraces, it's the perfect spot to relax and enjoy the sea views. Boat tours offer a

unique perspective of the coastline and a chance to spot dolphins and whales in their natural habitat.
- **Luxury Marina:** Adjacent to the fishing harbor lies Puerto de Mogán's luxurious marina. Marvel at sleek yachts and catamarans moored alongside traditional fishing boats, creating a captivating contrast. Upscale restaurants and designer boutiques cater to a discerning clientele, offering a touch of luxury to your island experience.
- **Relaxation by the Beach:** Escape to the golden sands of Playa de Mogán, a sheltered cove protected by rock formations. Rent a sun lounger and umbrella and soak up the warm sunshine, or take a refreshing dip in the crystal-clear waters. For the more adventurous, water sports rentals offer opportunities for kayaking, stand-up paddleboarding, or snorkeling in the vibrant underwater world.
- **Explore the Town:** Venture beyond the harbor and explore the charming streets of Puerto de Mogán. Wander through a maze of whitewashed houses adorned with vibrant bougainvillea flowers, and discover local shops selling handcrafted souvenirs and Canarian delicacies. Don't miss the opportunity to sample fresh seafood at a waterfront restaurant, savoring the flavors of the island while enjoying the idyllic setting.

Combining these Day Trips:

- **Arucas & Teror:** These two charming towns are located close together, making them ideal for a combined day trip. Start your morning exploring the vibrant streets of Arucas, indulging in a rum tasting at the distillery, and marveling at the colonial architecture. In the afternoon, head to Teror to witness the Basilica del Pino and wander through the flower-adorned streets, enjoying the tranquil mountain atmosphere.
- **Bandama Caldera & Puerto de Mogán:** Combine a thrilling hike to the rim of the Bandama Caldera with a relaxing afternoon in the charming Puerto de Mogán. The contrasting landscapes offer a diverse experience – a morning exploring the volcanic wonders and an afternoon soaking up the sun and laid-back vibes of the coastal village.

7. Stargazing Paradise:

Las Palmas, with its minimal light pollution, boasts some of the clearest night skies in Europe. Imagine escaping the city lights and gazing upon a breathtaking celestial spectacle. Join a guided stargazing tour led by experienced astronomers who will help you identify constellations, planets, and even distant galaxies.

Alternatively, head to a secluded beach away from the city center, spread out a blanket, and marvel at the Milky Way stretching across the vast expanse of the night sky. This unforgettable experience will leave you feeling humbled by the universe's grandeur.

8. A Shopaholic's Paradise:

Las Palmas caters to every shopping whim, from traditional Canarian crafts to high-end designer stores. Wander through the bustling Mercado Central de Las Palmas and unearth unique souvenirs like hand-embroidered linens, locally-made pottery, and volcanic rock jewelry.

The Triana neighborhood boasts a vibrant shopping scene, with a mix of international brands and independent boutiques. Don't miss Calle Mayor de Triana, a pedestrianized street lined with shops selling everything from clothing and accessories to homeware and souvenirs.

For a touch of luxury, head to Las Arenas Shopping Center, featuring high-end designer stores and a variety of restaurants and cafes. No matter your budget or taste, Las Palmas offers a rewarding shopping experience.

9. Beyond the Beach:

Las Palmas caters not only to beach bums but also to active travelers seeking adventure. Surfing enthusiasts can catch waves along the shores of Las Canteras Beach, while windsurfers and kitesurfers can test their skills at Playa del Inglés, located south of the city.

For a scenic hike, lace up your boots and explore the Tamadaba National Park, offering breathtaking mountain trails and diverse ecosystems. Alternatively, rent a bicycle and explore the city's well-maintained coastal bike paths, enjoying the ocean breeze and stunning views.

10. Las Palmas After Dark

As the sun sets and the city lights twinkle to life, Las Palmas transforms into a vibrant hub of nightlife. Whether you crave lively bars with pulsating music or trendy rooftop bars with breathtaking views, the city caters to every mood.

- **Tapas & Cocktails:** Start your evening with a tapas crawl through the Vegueta district, sampling delicious small plates and indulging in refreshing cocktails at charming bars with a local atmosphere.
- **Live Music Bars:** Immerse yourself in the city's vibrant music scene by visiting a live music bar. Enjoy genres ranging from traditional Canarian music to energetic salsa bands or international DJs spinning tunes until the early hours.
- **Beachfront Bars & Clubs:** Head to the Playa de Las Canteras promenade and soak up the lively atmosphere. Beachfront bars offer stunning ocean views and a relaxed vibe, while trendy clubs pulsate with music and cater to those seeking a night of dancing.
- **Casino Games & Nightclubs:** Las Palmas offers a few casinos for those who enjoy trying their luck at classic games like blackjack and roulette. For a more high-energy experience, nightclubs with international DJs cater to a party crowd.

Additional Tips for Nightlife in Las Palmas:

- **Dress code:** The dress code in most bars and clubs is casual, though some upscale establishments may require smarter attire.
- **Nightlife Areas:** Popular nightlife areas include Vegueta district, Playa de Las Canteras promenade, and Playa de Las Alcaravaneras.

- **Transportation:** Las Palmas has a reliable taxi service and public buses operate until late. Consider ridesharing apps for convenient transportation options.
- **Safety:** Las Palmas is generally a safe city, but it's always wise to be aware of your surroundings and avoid secluded areas at night.

Las Palmas offers something for everyone, whether you're a history buff, a beach lover, a cultural enthusiast, or a party animal. So, pack your bags, embrace the vibrant energy of this captivating city, and embark on an unforgettable adventure in the heart of Gran Canaria.

Unveiling the Island's Diverse Landscapes:

Gran Canaria, often referred to as a "miniature continent" due to its diverse landscapes, offers a feast for the senses beyond its stunning beaches. Imagine yourself venturing beyond the city limits, where dramatic mountains pierce the sky, volcanic craters whisper tales of fiery eruptions, and verdant valleys cradle charming villages steeped in history. Lace up your hiking boots, rent a car, or join a guided tour – Gran Canaria's breathtaking beauty awaits exploration.

1. The Tamadaba National Park

Located in the northwestern part of the island, Tamadaba National Park is a haven for nature lovers and outdoor enthusiasts. Imagine yourself trekking through a dense pine forest, the air crisp and clean, sunlight dappling through the canopy. Listen to the melodic chirping of birds and the rustling of leaves underfoot as you immerse yourself in the tranquility of this protected area.

- **Challenging Ascents & Breathtaking Views:** Tamadaba National Park caters to all levels of hikers. For seasoned adventurers, challenging ascents like Pico de la Cruz de Tejeda offer panoramic vistas that stretch across the entire northwest coast, with breathtaking views of the island's volcanic peaks and the shimmering ocean beyond. For a less strenuous option, choose a shorter trail that meanders through valleys, revealing hidden waterfalls and lush vegetation.

- **A Glimpse into the Past:** Keep an eye out for ancient pathways used by the indigenous Guanches, the island's first inhabitants. These pre-Hispanic trails, known as "caminos reales" (royal roads), offer a glimpse into the island's fascinating history and the ingenuity of its early people.
- **A Sanctuary for Wildlife:** Tamadaba National Park is a haven for diverse flora and fauna. Look out for playful rabbits darting through the undergrowth and keep your eyes peeled for endemic bird species like the blue chaffinch and the Berthelot's pipit. With a little luck, you might even spot a majestic Bonelli's eagle soaring above the trees.

2. The Bandama Caldera

Step back in time and explore the dramatic Bandama Caldera, a colossal natural wonder formed by a collapsed volcanic crater millions of years ago. Imagine standing at the rim of this awe-inspiring formation, gazing down at the vast caldera floor stretching out before you. The dramatic landscape, with its steep cliffs and verdant vegetation clinging to the slopes, creates an atmosphere of raw, untamed beauty.

- **Moderate Hikes & Stunning Views:** Hiking trails lead to the rim of the caldera, offering a rewarding experience for moderate walkers. As you ascend, the vegetation changes, with scrubland giving way to volcanic rock formations. Reaching the summit rewards you with breathtaking panoramic views of the surrounding landscapes, including the distant ocean and the island's other volcanic peaks.
- **A Geological Marvel:** The Bandama Caldera offers a fascinating glimpse into the island's volcanic past. Informative panels along the hiking trail explain the geological processes that shaped this natural wonder. Observe the volcanic rock formations, each with its unique features, and imagine the immense power of the eruption that created this awe-inspiring landscape.
- **Wine Tasting with a View:** After your invigorating hike, consider visiting the nearby Villa Bandama Golf Resort. Indulge in a delicious meal or a glass

of locally produced Canarian wine while soaking up the breathtaking panorama of the Bandama Caldera from a luxurious setting.

3. The Fataga Valley

Escape the coastal crowds and delve into the lush oasis of the Fataga Valley, often referred to as the "Valley of a Thousand Palms." Imagine yourself driving through a verdant canyon, flanked by towering cliffs and dotted with traditional whitewashed villages nestled amidst palm groves. The gentle murmur of streams and the vibrant green of the vegetation create a sense of tranquility and peace.

- **Hiking & Biking Trails:** The Fataga Valley boasts a network of well-maintained hiking and biking trails, catering to all levels of fitness. For a leisurely stroll, follow the gentle stream alongside charming villages, enjoying the scenery and the refreshing scent of citrus trees. For the more adventurous, challenging hikes lead to hidden waterfalls and breathtaking viewpoints.
- **Charming Villages:** Dotted throughout the Fataga Valley are picturesque villages that seem to have frozen in time. Explore quaint settlements like Fataga, Arteara, and San Bartolomé de Tirajana, where traditional Canarian architecture reigns supreme. Stroll through cobbled streets, admire whitewashed houses adorned with colorful flowers, and soak up the laid-back atmosphere of these hidden gems.
- **Local Produce & Gastronomy:** Savor the flavors of Gran Canaria in the Fataga Valley. Stop at roadside stalls selling fresh fruits and vegetables grown in the fertile soil, or visit local shops offering homemade jams, honey, and traditional cheeses. Indulge in a delicious lunch at a charming restaurant with a terrace overlooking the valley, where you can sample regional specialties like "papas arrugadas" (wrinkled potatoes) with mojo sauces, fresh seafood dishes, and locally produced wines.

4. The Guayadeque Ravine

Venture into the heart of Gran Canaria's ancient history by exploring the Guayadeque Ravine, a dramatic canyon carved by time and erosion. Imagine yourself walking through a landscape dotted with prehistoric cave dwellings inhabited by the island's first inhabitants, the Guanches, centuries ago.

- **A Window into the Guanche World:** Explore reconstructed Guanche dwellings, meticulously recreated to offer a glimpse into their way of life. See how they used natural caves for shelter, storage, and even religious ceremonies. Learn about their unique culture, social structures, and ingenious methods of adapting to the island's environment.
- **A Hike Through History:** Hiking trails wind through the Guayadeque Ravine, offering stunning views of the canyon walls and the surrounding landscapes. As you walk, keep an eye out for the "cenobio de Guayadeque," a complex of artificial caves believed to have been used for religious purposes. Imagine the whispers of the past echoing through these ancient dwellings, adding a sense of mystery to your exploration.
- **A Touch of Modernity:** While steeped in history, the Guayadeque Ravine also boasts some modern-day surprises. Dotted throughout the canyon are whitewashed houses built into the cliffs, creating a unique blend of ancient and contemporary living. You might even encounter local artisans selling handcrafted souvenirs, adding a touch of vibrancy to the historical setting.

5. The Village of Tejeda

Nestled amidst the highest peaks of Gran Canaria lies the charming village of Tejeda, often referred to as "the Roof of Gran Canaria." Imagine yourself driving along winding roads through a landscape of pine forests and dramatic rock formations, culminating in this idyllic mountain village. The crisp mountain air, breathtaking scenery, and tranquil atmosphere offer a welcome respite from the coastal heat.

- **A Paradise for Hikers:** Tejeda serves as a fantastic base for exploring the surrounding peaks. Hiking trails of varying difficulty levels cater to all types

of adventurers. For a moderate challenge, embark on a hike to Cruz de Tejeda, the highest point on the island, and be rewarded with panoramic vistas that stretch across the entire island.
- **Almonds Take Center Stage:** Tejeda is renowned for its almond groves, boasting the largest almond production on the island. Visit during the almond blossom season in February, and witness the landscape transformed into a sea of delicate pink and white flowers, creating a breathtaking spectacle. Sample local delicacies like almond marzipan and almond liqueur, a true taste of Tejeda's unique charm.
- **A Cultural Experience:** Immerse yourself in the local culture by visiting the village's main square, Plaza de Santa Lucia. Browse through stalls selling traditional crafts and engage with friendly locals. Don't miss the opportunity to try "bienmesabe," a delicious Canarian dessert made with almonds, honey, and eggs – a perfect way to end your exploration of this hidden gem.

Chasing Stars Under the Milky Way

Gran Canaria, with minimal light pollution, boasts some of the clearest night skies in Europe. Imagine yourself escaping the city lights and venturing into the heart of a nature reserve, a blanket spread beneath you, and a sky ablaze with a million twinkling stars. The Milky Way stretches across the vast expanse above you, while constellations come alive, each with its own captivating story.

- **Stargazing Tours:** For an unforgettable experience, join a guided stargazing tour. Expert astronomers will guide you through the night sky, pointing out constellations, planets, and even distant galaxies through powerful telescopes. Learn about the fascinating history of astronomy, the myths and legends associated with the stars, and gain a newfound appreciation for the vastness of the universe.
- **Finding the Perfect Spot:** If you prefer a more independent experience, head to a secluded beach or a designated stargazing spot away from the city lights. Look for areas with minimal light pollution, such as nature reserves or designated viewpoints in the mountains. Download a stargazing app to help you identify celestial objects and enhance your experience.

- **A Moment of Reflection:** As you gaze upon the breathtaking night sky, a sense of awe and wonder washes over you. The vastness of space puts your worries into perspective and ignites a sense of curiosity about the universe's mysteries. This experience is a perfect way to reconnect with nature and create a lasting memory of your Gran Canarian adventure.

Insider Tips for Exploring Gran Canaria's Landscapes:

- **Pack for All Weather Conditions:** Gran Canaria's diverse landscapes experience varying microclimates. Pack layers even when visiting coastal areas, as temperatures can drop significantly in the mountains. Don't forget sunscreen, sunglasses, and a hat for sun protection, especially during the summer months.
- **Respect the Environment:** Leave no trace behind when exploring Gran Canaria's natural beauty. Stick to designated trails, dispose of waste responsibly, and avoid disturbing wildlife. Help preserve the island's pristine landscapes for future generations to enjoy.
- **Comfortable Footwear:** Many of Gran Canaria's landscapes are best explored on foot. Invest in a good pair of hiking boots that provide ankle support and good traction, especially for challenging hikes.
- **Safety First:** Always inform someone of your planned route, especially when venturing into remote areas. Carry a map and compass, and be aware of potential hazards like loose rocks or sudden weather changes.
- **Embrace the Local Culture:** Stop by a local grocery store and stock up on snacks and drinks for your adventures. Support local artisans by purchasing handcrafted souvenirs. Learning a few basic Spanish phrases will go a long way in connecting with the friendly locals.

Gran Canaria isn't just a beach destination; it's a captivating island waiting to be explored. From dramatic volcanic craters and verdant valleys to charming mountain villages and star-studded night skies, Gran Canaria offers a diverse tapestry of landscapes that will leave you breathless. So, pack your bags, embrace your sense of adventure, and embark on a journey to unveil the hidden wonders of this Canary Island paradise. You'll return home with a collection of unforgettable memories and a newfound appreciation for Gran Canaria's natural beauty and rich cultural heritage.

Exploring the Coast:

Gran Canaria, a jewel in the Canary Islands crown, boasts a coastline as diverse as its landscapes. Imagine yourself basking under the warm Canarian sun, the gentle ocean breeze caressing your skin, and the turquoise waters inviting you for a refreshing dip. Whether you crave the vibrant energy of a bustling resort or seek the tranquility of a secluded cove, Gran Canaria's beaches cater to every desire. So, pack your swimsuit, sunscreen, and a sense of adventure – let's embark on a coastal exploration!

1. The Beaches of the South

The southern shores of Gran Canaria are synonymous with sunshine, golden sands, and a buzzing holiday atmosphere. Here, popular resorts like Playa del Inglés, Maspalomas, and Puerto Rico offer a plethora of activities, amenities, and entertainment options for all ages.

- **Playa del Inglés – A Lively Hub:** Imagine yourself strolling along the seemingly endless golden sands of Playa del Inglés, one of the most popular beaches on the island. The vibrant atmosphere is contagious, with beach bars pumping out music, watersports vendors offering an array of activities, and families frolicking in the shallows. For the adventurous, thrilling windsurfing and kitesurfing conditions await, while those seeking relaxation can rent sun loungers and umbrellas and soak up the sun. After sunset, the lively nightlife scene takes over, with bars and restaurants catering to every taste.
- **Maspalomas – Dunes and Beach Bliss:** Escape to the unique landscape of Maspalomas, where the golden sands meet a breathtaking expanse of rolling dunes. Imagine yourself feeling the soft sand between your toes as you explore the Maspalomas Dunes, a designated Natural Reserve offering a unique desert-like experience. For a refreshing dip, head to the Playa del

Inglés beach extension, a sheltered cove with calm waters perfect for swimming and sunbathing. End your day with a romantic stroll along the beach promenade, watching the sunset paint the sky in vibrant hues.
- **Puerto Rico – Family Fun in the Sun:** Picture yourself nestled on a sun lounger on the golden sands of Puerto Rico's beach, watching your children build sandcastles and splash in the calm waters. This family-friendly resort offers a relaxed atmosphere with plenty of amenities to keep everyone entertained. Enjoy a variety of watersports like kayaking, paddleboarding, or banana boat rides. Explore the bustling marina, teeming with luxurious yachts and offering boat trips for dolphin and whale watching. In the evening, indulge in a delicious seafood meal at a beachfront restaurant, enjoying the cool evening breeze and the twinkling lights of the resort.

2. The Diverse Beaches of the West

The west coast of Gran Canaria offers a treasure trove of hidden coves and secluded beaches, ideal for those seeking a more tranquil escape. Imagine yourself swimming in crystal-clear waters, surrounded by dramatic cliffs, and breathing in the fresh ocean air. Here are a few hidden gems waiting to be discovered:

- **Playa de Mogán – Tranquility by Design:** Escape to the idyllic setting of Puerto de Mogán, a charming fishing village nestled on the southwest coast. Its main beach, Playa de Mogán, is a haven for relaxation. Imagine yourself luxuriating on sun loungers, surrounded by lush vegetation and sheltered from the wind by the harbor. Rent a kayak or paddleboard and explore the calm waters, marveling at the colorful fish darting around the rocky outcrops. Indulge in a gourmet meal at a beachfront restaurant, savoring fresh seafood while soaking up the idyllic atmosphere.
- **Guigui Beach – A Hike and a Reward:** For the adventurous soul, Guigui Beach offers a unique experience. Accessible only by foot or boat, this secluded cove is a true hidden gem. Imagine embarking on a scenic hike along a coastal path, the rugged cliffs offering breathtaking ocean views. Reaching the beach is a reward in itself – pristine golden sands bathed in turquoise waters, untouched by development, offer a sense of complete

peace and tranquility. Pack a picnic lunch and spend the day soaking up the sun and the secluded beauty of this natural wonder.
- **Agaete Natural Pools – Volcanic Charm:** Located on the northwest coast, the Agaete Natural Pools offer a unique swimming experience. Imagine yourself surrounded by volcanic rock formations that have been sculpted by the waves, creating a series of natural pools filled with crystal-clear seawater. Relax on the volcanic rock platforms, soak up the sun, and enjoy the refreshing dip in these naturally formed pools. Explore the charming town of Agaete, known for its coffee plantations and laid-back atmosphere, to complete your experience.

3. The Beaches of the South East

The southeastern shores of Gran Canaria offer a haven for those seeking a touch of luxury and exclusivity. Imagine yourself basking on pristine white sand beaches, pampered by attentive staff at five-star resorts, and enjoying world-class amenities. Here are a couple of exquisite options:

- **Meloneras – Designer Chic and Pristine Sands:** Picture yourself strolling along the pristine white sand beach of Meloneras, a resort renowned for its luxurious hotels, designer boutiques, and high-end restaurants. Relax on comfortable sun loungers and soak up the sun, indulging in personalized service from beach attendants. For a touch of adventure, try your hand at jet skiing or parasailing, enjoying the thrill of skimming across the turquoise waters. In the evening, indulge in a gourmet dining experience at a beachfront restaurant, savoring exquisite cuisine under the starlit sky.
- **Pasito Blanco – Yachting Paradise and Secluded Bliss:** Escape to the tranquil setting of Pasito Blanco, a haven for luxury yachts and discerning travelers. Imagine yourself nestled on a sun lounger on the secluded beach of Playa de Tauro, a sheltered cove with calm waters ideal for swimming and snorkeling. For the active traveler, world-class diving opportunities await, with vibrant coral reefs teeming with marine life to explore. In the afternoon, rent a boat and explore the dramatic coastline, spotting playful dolphins and majestic whales in their natural habitat. As the sun dips below

the horizon, enjoy a sundowner cocktail at a chic beach bar, soaking up the luxurious atmosphere of Pasito Blanco.

4. Unveiling the North:

The northern shores of Gran Canaria offer a contrasting experience, showcasing the island's rugged beauty and powerful waves. Imagine yourself standing on a black volcanic sand beach, the wind whipping through your hair, and the vast expanse of the Atlantic Ocean stretching out before you. This is a place for surfers, nature enthusiasts, and those seeking a more raw and untamed coastal experience.

- **Las Canteras Beach – A City Oasis:** Located in the heart of Las Palmas, the capital city, Las Canteras Beach offers a convenient option for urban explorers. Imagine yourself strolling along the golden sand beach, a vibrant promenade lined with cafes and restaurants buzzing with activity. The beach itself is divided into two sections – La Playa de la Cícer (Beach of the Chickpeas) with calm waters perfect for families, and La Playa de las Alcaravaneras (Beach of the Sandpipers) favored by surfers for its challenging waves. Enjoy a refreshing swim, try your hand at surfing lessons, or simply relax and soak up the lively atmosphere.
- **Gáldar – A Historical Journey and Dramatic Coastline:** Combine your beach experience with a historical adventure in Gáldar, a town steeped in ancient history. Imagine yourself exploring the archaeological site of La Cueva Pintada (The Painted Cave), a fascinating glimpse into the lives of the island's first inhabitants. Afterward, head to the dramatic black sand beach of Puerto de Sardina, a haven for surfers and strong swimmers. The powerful waves and stunning backdrop of volcanic cliffs create a sense of raw, untamed beauty. Enjoy a delicious seafood lunch at a beachfront restaurant, savoring fresh flavors while admiring the dramatic coastline.
- **Agaete Valley – Secluded Beaches and Hidden Gems:** Venture beyond the main coastal road and discover the hidden gem of the Agaete Valley, nestled on the northwest coast. Imagine yourself exploring a lush valley dotted with banana plantations and charming villages. Follow a winding path and discover secluded coves like Playa de las Nieves (Beach of the Snows), a

tranquil haven with pristine white sand and crystal-clear waters. For a unique experience, rent a kayak and explore the hidden coves and dramatic rock formations along the coastline, soaking up the secluded beauty of this untouched paradise.

Gran Canaria's Coastal Tapestry: Awaits Your Exploration

From the bustling resorts of the south to the secluded coves of the west and north, Gran Canaria's coastline offers something for every traveler. Whether you crave sun-drenched relaxation, thrilling water sports, or a touch of luxury, this captivating island will not disappoint. So, pack your swimsuit, grab your beach towel, and embark on an unforgettable coastal adventure in Gran Canaria! Let the sun kiss your skin, the waves lull you into a state of relaxation, and the beauty of the island's diverse beaches create memories that will last a lifetime.

Adventure Activities: Hiking, cycling, water sports, and exploring hidden gems

Gran Canaria isn't just a haven for sunbathers and beach bums. Beneath its golden sands and turquoise waters lies a vibrant tapestry of adventure waiting to be explored. Lace up your hiking boots, grab your bike, or prepare to get wet – a world of thrilling activities awaits the intrepid traveler. Let's delve into the heart of Gran Canaria's adventurous spirit:

1. Hiking Through Time: Unveiling the Island's Diverse Landscapes

Strap on your backpack and lace up your hiking boots because Gran Canaria's dramatic landscapes are begging to be explored on foot. Imagine yourself traversing through lush valleys, ascending volcanic peaks, and following ancient pathways used by the island's first inhabitants. Here are a few unforgettable hiking trails:

- **Tamadaba National Park - A Journey Through a Pine Forest:** Breathe in the crisp mountain air as you trek through the dense pine forests of Tamadaba National Park. Imagine sunlight dappling through the canopy, casting a magical glow on the forest floor. Listen to the melodic chirping of birds and the rustling of leaves as you immerse yourself in the tranquility of this protected area. Challenging ascents like Pico de la Cruz de Tejeda reward you with panoramic vistas that stretch across the entire northwest coast, while shorter trails offer a more leisurely exploration of hidden waterfalls and verdant valleys.
- **The Bandama Caldera - A Hike into a Volcanic Crater:** Step back in time and explore the dramatic Bandama Caldera, a colossal natural wonder formed by a collapsed volcanic crater millions of years ago. Imagine yourself standing at the rim of this awe-inspiring formation, gazing down at the vast caldera floor stretching out before you. Moderate hikes lead to the rim, offering stunning views of the surrounding landscapes. As you ascend, the vegetation changes, with scrubland giving way to volcanic rock formations. Keep an eye out for informative panels along the trail that explain the geological processes that shaped this natural wonder. After your invigorating hike, consider visiting the nearby Villa Bandama Golf Resort. Indulge in a delicious meal or a glass of locally produced Canarian wine while soaking up the breathtaking panorama from a luxurious setting.
- **The Fataga Valley - A Lush Oasis Beckons:** Escape the coastal crowds and delve into the lush oasis of the Fataga Valley, often referred to as the "Valley of a Thousand Palms." Picture yourself driving through a verdant canyon flanked by towering cliffs and dotted with traditional whitewashed villages nestled amidst palm groves. The gentle murmur of streams and the vibrant green of the vegetation create a sense of tranquility and peace. Hike or bike through the valley, following gentle streams alongside charming villages. For a more challenging option, ascend to hidden waterfalls and breathtaking viewpoints. Don't miss the opportunity to savor the flavors of Gran Canaria by stopping at roadside stalls selling fresh fruits and vegetables grown in the fertile soil or indulging in a delicious lunch at a charming restaurant overlooking the valley.

2. Two Wheels, Endless Exploration: Cycling Adventures on Gran Canaria

Gran Canaria offers a paradise for cyclists, with routes catering to all levels and preferences. Imagine yourself cruising along scenic coastal roads, feeling the wind in your hair and the invigorating ocean spray on your face. Alternatively, challenge yourself on demanding climbs through mountainous terrain and reward yourself with breathtaking panoramas. Here are some cycling experiences to consider:

- **Coastal Cruises:** For a relaxed ride, choose a coastal route. Imagine yourself cycling along dedicated bike paths that hug the coastline, offering stunning views of secluded coves, dramatic cliffs, and the sparkling turquoise ocean. Stop for a refreshing dip at a hidden beach or explore charming fishing villages along the way. Popular options include the Playa del Inglés to Maspalomas route, offering a flat and scenic ride, or the more challenging Mogán coastal route with its rolling hills and breathtaking vistas.
- **Mountain Challenges:** For seasoned cyclists seeking a challenge, Gran Canaria boasts a network of demanding mountain climbs. Imagine yourself conquering steep inclines, feeling your legs burn with exertion, and then reaching a summit and being rewarded with panoramic vistas that stretch across the entire island. Popular climbs include the ascent to Pico de las Nieves, the island's highest peak, or the challenging route from Fataga Valley to Degollada de la Cazuela, offering breathtaking views of the surrounding valleys.
- **Guided Tours:** If you're unfamiliar with the island or prefer a more structured experience, consider joining a guided cycling tour. These tours cater to all levels and offer a safe and enjoyable way to explore the island's diverse landscapes. Expert guides will lead you through scenic routes, share interesting facts about the island's history and culture, and ensure you have a memorable cycling adventure.

3. Making Waves: Water Sports Paradise Awaits

Gran Canaria's sparkling turquoise waters are a playground for water sports enthusiasts. Whether you're a seasoned surfer, a curious snorkeler, or simply want to try something new, there's an activity waiting to get your adrenaline pumping or allow you to explore the underwater world.

- **Surfing Paradise:** Gran Canaria's north and west coasts are renowned for their consistent waves, attracting surfers from all over the world. Imagine yourself paddling out to catch a wave, feeling the thrill of gliding across the water and the power of the ocean beneath you. Popular surf spots include Playa del Inglés, Aguineguín, and Las Canteras Beach, offering waves for all skill levels. If you're a beginner, consider taking surf lessons from experienced instructors who will guide you through the basics and get you up and riding in no time.
- **Stand Up Paddleboarding (SUP):** For a more relaxed experience on the water, try stand-up paddleboarding (SUP). Imagine yourself standing on a large, stable board, gliding effortlessly across the calm waters. Explore hidden coves inaccessible by land, spot colorful fish in crystal-clear waters, or simply enjoy the peace and tranquility of being out on the ocean. SUP is a fantastic way to explore the coastline from a different perspective and enjoy a low-impact workout at the same time. Popular spots for SUP include the calm waters of Puerto de Mogán, the protected bay of Anfi del Mar, and the Agaete Natural Pools.
- **Scuba Diving & Snorkeling:** Dive into a world of vibrant colors and fascinating marine life by exploring Gran Canaria's underwater world. Imagine yourself swimming alongside schools of colorful fish, encountering majestic stingrays, or even spotting playful dolphins. Gran Canaria boasts several dive sites, catering to both beginners and experienced divers. Explore underwater volcanic formations, shipwrecks teeming with marine life, and coral reefs bursting with color. For a more accessible underwater experience, try snorkeling. Explore the shallow waters of hidden coves, observe a variety of fish species in their natural habitat, and marvel at the beauty of the underwater world without needing special equipment.

4. Beyond the Tourist Trail

Gran Canaria offers more than just popular resorts and well-marked trails. For the adventurous traveler, venturing beyond the beaten track unveils hidden gems and unique experiences. Imagine yourself exploring charming villages untouched by mass tourism, discovering ancient caves inhabited by the island's first inhabitants, or stumbling upon breathtaking natural wonders. Let's explore a few off-the-beaten-path adventures:

- **The Cactualdea Park:** Immerse yourself in a world of exotic cacti and succulents at the Cactualdea Park, a botanical garden located near Puerto Rico. Imagine yourself strolling through themed gardens showcasing a vast collection of cacti from around the world, some towering specimens reaching impressive heights. Learn about the unique adaptations of these desert plants and marvel at the vibrant colors and intricate shapes of the various species. After exploring the park, enjoy a breathtaking panoramic view of the Puerto Rico resort from a dedicated viewpoint.

Unleashing Your Inner Explorer:

Gran Canaria is a playground for adventurers of all kinds. From challenging hikes and thrilling water sports to discovering ancient secrets and hidden gems, the island offers endless opportunities to push your limits and create unforgettable memories. So, pack your sense of adventure, lace up your boots, grab your gear, and embark on a journey to unveil the hidden wonders of Gran Canaria!

Part 3: Tantalize Your Taste Buds: Gran Canaria's Culinary Delights

A Gastronomic Journey: Exploring Local Cuisine

Gran Canaria isn't just a feast for the eyes; it's a tantalizing treat for the taste buds as well. Imagine yourself embarking on a culinary adventure, savoring traditional dishes bursting with fresh, local flavors, and indulging in the unique gastronomy that reflects the island's rich cultural heritage. From fresh seafood caught just hours before landing on your plate to comforting stews simmered in volcanic heat and locally produced wines, Gran Canaria's cuisine is a symphony of taste and tradition waiting to be explored.

1. Embracing Canarian Classics

Canarian cuisine is a vibrant tapestry woven from influences brought by the island's indigenous inhabitants, the Guanches, Spanish settlers, and explorers from across the Atlantic. Imagine yourself sitting at a charming restaurant with a checkered tablecloth and a view of the ocean, ready to embark on a culinary journey through time. Here are some quintessential Canarian dishes you simply must try:

- **Papas Arrugadas con Mojo:** This iconic dish is a staple of Canarian cuisine. Imagine perfectly wrinkled potatoes, boiled in very salty water, served piping hot with two types of mojo sauce – a spicy red mojo rojo and a more mellow green mojo verde made with coriander and parsley. The simplicity of this dish allows the natural flavor of the potatoes to shine, perfectly complemented by the contrasting flavors of the mojo sauces. Dip, savor, and repeat – it's a Canarian tradition!

- **Gofio:** A staple food of the Guanches, gofio is a roasted and ground mixture of various grains, typically barley, wheat, or maize. Imagine yourself trying gofio escaldado, a porridge-like dish made with gofio, water, and a touch of salt. This simple yet nutritious dish is a testament to the resourcefulness of the island's indigenous people. Gofio can also be incorporated into other dishes, adding a unique nutty flavor and a textural contrast.
- **Rancho Canario:** This hearty stew is a comforting staple, perfect for a cool evening. Imagine a rich broth simmered with various meats like chicken, pork, or rabbit, along with vegetables like potatoes, carrots, and green beans. The addition of chickpeas adds protein and texture, while a touch of saffron infuses the dish with a delicate aroma. Rancho Canario is a true comfort food, perfect for warming you up from the inside out.

2. Fresh from the Ocean to Your Plate

The crystal-clear waters surrounding Gran Canaria are a treasure trove of fresh fish and seafood. Imagine yourself dining at a waterfront restaurant, the gentle sea breeze carrying the scent of salt and the sound of waves crashing against the shore as you savor the bounty of the ocean. Here are some local seafood specialties you can't miss:

- **Pescado a la Parrilla:** Simplicity reigns supreme when it comes to fresh fish in Gran Canaria. Imagine a whole fish, perfectly grilled over hot coals, seasoned with just a touch of salt and olive oil. The result? Perfectly cooked fish with a crispy skin and succulent flesh, allowing the natural flavor of the ocean to shine through. This dish is often served with papas arrugadas and mojo sauces, creating a perfectly balanced and delicious meal.
- **Caldo de Pescado:** For a taste of the sea in a comforting bowl, try caldo de pescado, a traditional fish stew. Imagine a rich and flavorful broth simmered with a variety of fish and shellfish, along with vegetables like potatoes, onions, and tomatoes. This hearty stew is a delicious way to warm up on a cool evening and savor the diverse flavors of the ocean.
- **Lapas y Almejas:** For a more casual seafood experience, head to a local tapas bar. Imagine yourself sharing plates of freshly caught limpets (lapas) and clams (almejas) grilled to perfection, their briny flavor a true taste of

the sea. Pair them with a glass of local white wine for an authentic Canarian culinary experience.

3. Exploring Island Specialties

Gran Canaria boasts a diverse landscape, and each region has its own unique culinary specialties that reflect the local ingredients and traditions. Venture beyond the main tourist areas and discover the hidden gems of Canarian cuisine:

- **Mojos in all their Glory:** While the classic red and green mojo sauces are ubiquitous, each region puts its own spin on them. Imagine yourself exploring the island and discovering variations like mojo picón, a spicy red mojo with a kick of chili peppers, or mojo Palmero, a milder version from La Palma island. Don't be afraid to experiment and find your favorite flavor combination!
- **Ropa Vieja:** This slow-cooked stew originates from Spain but has become a beloved dish in Gran Canaria with its own unique twist. Imagine yourself digging into a comforting bowl of ropa vieja, featuring tender shredded beef simmered in a rich tomato and vegetable sauce. The addition of local spices like cumin and paprika adds a depth of flavor, while green peas and peppers provide pops of color and freshness. This hearty dish is typically served with rice or potatoes, making it a perfect lunch or dinner option.
- **Queso Asado con Mojo:** Cheese lovers, rejoice! Queso Asado con Mojo is a simple yet satisfying dish showcasing the island's local cheeses. Imagine yourself savoring a warm slice of Canarian cheese, typically goat or sheep's milk cheese, grilled to perfection until slightly melted and golden brown. Drizzle it with your favorite mojo sauce for a flavor explosion – the creamy cheese perfectly complements the contrasting tangy or spicy notes of the mojo. This dish is often enjoyed as an appetizer or a light lunch with a glass of local wine.
- **Bienmesabe:** Save room for dessert because Gran Canaria offers a delightful selection of sweet treats. Imagine indulging in bienmesabe, a traditional Canarian almond dessert. This rich and creamy concoction is made with almonds, honey, eggs, and a touch of lemon zest. The result? A

heavenly combination of sweet and nutty flavors with a smooth and luxurious texture. Bienmesabe is the perfect way to end a delicious meal and experience a taste of Canarian tradition.

A Culinary Adventure Awaits:

Gran Canaria's cuisine is more than just food; it's a cultural experience that connects you to the island's history, traditions, and the bounty of its natural environment. So, embark on a culinary adventure, savor the fresh flavors, and discover the hidden gems of Canarian gastronomy. From traditional stews simmered in volcanic heat to the freshest seafood caught just hours before landing on your plate, Gran Canaria's cuisine is a symphony of taste waiting to be explored. Buen provecho (enjoy your meal)!

Best Local Drinks to Savor

No culinary adventure is complete without exploring the local libations. Imagine yourself relaxing on a sun-drenched terrace, enjoying breathtaking ocean views, and sipping on a refreshing beverage that perfectly complements the delicious Canarian cuisine. Gran Canaria offers a diverse selection of drinks, from locally produced wines to unique liqueurs and thirst-quenching concoctions. So, raise a glass and embark on a journey of flavor discovery!

1. Wines of Gran Canaria

The volcanic soils and warm climate of Gran Canaria create ideal conditions for grape cultivation, resulting in a unique and flavorful selection of local wines. Imagine yourself visiting a traditional bodega (winery) nestled amidst rolling vineyards, learning about the island's winemaking process, and indulging in a tasting experience. Here are some of the local grape varieties and wines you should try:

- **Listán Negro & Blanco:** These indigenous grape varieties are the heart and soul of Canarian wines. Imagine yourself sipping on a glass of Listán Negro, a light-bodied red wine with notes of red berries and a hint of spice. For a refreshing white wine experience, try Listán Blanco, known for its crisp acidity, citrusy aromas, and mineral notes. These versatile wines pair beautifully with a variety of Canarian dishes, from seafood to stews.
- **Malvasía Volcanica:** This aromatic white wine is a true expression of Gran Canaria's volcanic terroir. Imagine the distinct aroma of volcanic ash mingling with notes of tropical fruits and honey on your nose. The first sip reveals a refreshing acidity balanced by a hint of sweetness, making it an ideal aperitif or a perfect companion to lighter seafood dishes.
- **Denomination of Origin Wines:** Gran Canaria boasts two Denominations of Origin (DO) - D.O. Valle de Güimar and D.O. Islas Canarias. Imagine yourself seeking out wines with these labels, ensuring you're experiencing the highest quality local production. These wines are subject to strict regulations, guaranteeing authenticity and a true taste of Gran Canaria's unique terroir.

2. Local Liqueurs to Discover

While wine reigns supreme, Gran Canaria offers a selection of potent and flavorful local liqueurs to tantalize your taste buds. Imagine yourself venturing into a traditional shop and browsing shelves lined with colorful bottles, each holding a unique spirit waiting to be discovered. Here are a few local liqueurs to add a fiery kick to your Canarian experience:

- **Ron Miel (Honey Rum):** This ubiquitous liqueur is as much a part of Canarian culture as papas arrugadas. Imagine yourself indulging in a shot of Ron Miel after a meal, the sweet honey flavor mingling with the warmth of the rum. Some restaurants leave a bottle on the table, allowing you to adjust the sweetness to your preference. While traditionally enjoyed neat, Ron Miel can also be incorporated into cocktails for a unique twist.
- **Arehucas Rum:** For a taste of history, explore the world of Arehucas Rum, the island's most renowned rum producer. Imagine yourself taking a tour of the Arehucas distillery, learning about the rum-making process from

sugarcane to barrel-aging. Sample a variety of rums, from light and airy white rums to aged dark rums with notes of caramel and oak.
- **Barraquito:** This layered coffee liqueur is a local favorite, perfect for a post-dinner pick-me-up. Imagine a visually stunning concoction – a base of condensed milk, followed by coffee liqueur, a layer of local aguardiente (a strong sugarcane spirit), and topped with a sprinkle of cinnamon. The sweetness of the condensed milk balances the bitterness of the coffee and the fiery kick of the aguardiente, creating a truly unique and delicious beverage.

3. Quenching Your Thirst: Refreshing Canarian Drinks

The warm Canarian climate demands refreshing beverages to keep you cool throughout the day. Imagine yourself exploring local markets and cafes, discovering a variety of thirst-quenching drinks that are as delicious as they are invigorating. Here are a few local non-alcoholic options to beat the heat:

- **Agua de Valencia:** This vibrant orange-hued drink is a festive and refreshing option. Imagine yourself sipping on a mixture of freshly squeezed orange juice, cava (Spanish sparkling wine), and a touch of sugar. This bubbly concoction is perfect for a midday pick-me-up or to share with friends during a celebratory toast.
- **Hierba Luisa Tea:** For a taste of pure relaxation, try hierba luisa tea. Imagine yourself savoring a cup of this fragrant herbal tea made with lemon verbena leaves. Known for its calming properties and refreshing flavor, hierba luisa tea is the perfect way to unwind after a day of exploring the island. You can find it hot or iced, catering to your preference. Many restaurants serve it complimentary after a meal, a delightful way to cleanse your palate and aid digestion.
- **Freshly Squeezed Juices:** Embrace the abundance of fresh fruits grown on the island by indulging in a glass of freshly squeezed juice. Imagine yourself stopping at a roadside stall or a local cafe and choosing from a variety of options like mango, papaya, guava, or a tropical blend. These vitamin-packed beverages are not only refreshing but also a healthy way to quench your thirst under the Canarian sun.

Beyond the Glass

Exploring local drinks in Gran Canaria goes beyond just the taste. It's about immersing yourself in the island's culture and traditions. Imagine yourself joining locals at a lively "guachinche," a traditional eatery often located in a garage or backyard. These rustic establishments offer a chance to sample homemade food and local wines at a fraction of the price of a restaurant. Be prepared for a lively atmosphere, friendly conversation, and a truly authentic Canarian experience.

Street Food and Markets:

Gran Canaria's culinary scene extends far beyond the menus of fancy restaurants. Imagine yourself immersing yourself in the vibrant energy of local markets and street food stalls, where the air is filled with enticing aromas, colorful displays tempt your taste buds, and friendly vendors share their culinary passion. Here's where you can truly experience the soul of Canarian cuisine, savoring fresh, local ingredients transformed into delicious and affordable bites.

1. Exploring Vibrant Markets

Gran Canaria boasts a network of bustling markets, each offering a unique sensory experience. Imagine yourself wandering through stalls overflowing with colorful fruits and vegetables, freshly caught seafood glistening on ice, and local artisans showcasing their handcrafted goods. Here are a few markets you can't miss:

Market: Mercado Central de Las Palmas

- **Location**: Plaza de la Feria, Las Palmas de Gran Canaria
- **Operating Days:** Monday-Saturday
- **Operating Hours:** 8:00 AM - 2:00 PM (closed on Sundays)

- **Specialties:** Fresh produce, local meats and cheeses, seafood, spices, flowers, souvenirs
- **Average Price Range:** Varies depending on the product
- **Tips for Bargaining:** Bargaining is not customary at established markets like this one. However, some vendors might offer small discounts if you purchase a larger quantity.

Must-Try: Immerse yourself in the colorful chaos of the Mercado Central de Las Palmas, the largest market on the island. Stroll past stalls overflowing with fresh, seasonal produce – plump tomatoes, exotic tropical fruits, and vibrant greens just picked from the local farms. Indulge in a selection of local cheeses, from the creamy Queso Majorero to the sharp Flor de Guía. For a true Canarian treat, try a "gofio escaldado," a simple yet flavorful dish made with roasted gofio (milled grain) and broth, often served with a touch of honey.

Market: Puerto de Mogán Market

- **Location:** Puerto de Mogán, Mogán Municipality
- **Operating Days:** Daily
- **Operating Hours:** Varies depending on the vendor, typically 10:00 AM - 6:00 PM
- **Specialties:** Fresh seafood, local fruits and vegetables, spices, handicrafts, souvenirs
- **Average Price Range:** Varies depending on the product
- **Tips for Bargaining:** Light bargaining might be possible, particularly at the end of the day or for larger purchases. Be polite and respectful while negotiating.

Must-Try: The picturesque Puerto de Mogán Market offers a delightful blend of fresh produce, local crafts, and delicious street food. Purchase the catch of the day from a friendly fishmonger, perhaps some vibrant red prawns or glistening sea bass. Explore the stalls overflowing with exotic fruits – guanabana with its spiky exterior and creamy interior, or the refreshing tang of passionfruit. For a quick bite, grab a "bocadillo," a simple yet satisfying sandwich filled with local ingredients like Spanish chorizo or almogrote (a spicy cheese spread).

2. Street Food Delights

The streets of Gran Canaria come alive with the tantalizing aroma of sizzling meats, freshly grilled vegetables, and traditional delicacies being prepared right before your eyes. Imagine yourself following your nose to colorful food stalls, each offering a unique and affordable culinary adventure. Here are some street food vendors you should seek out:

Vendor: Don Pepe - Churros

- **Location:** Playa del Inglés Promenade, Maspalomas
- **Operating Hours:** Afternoon and evening (hours may vary depending on the season)
- **Specialty Dish:** Churros (fried dough pastries)
- **Average Cost:** €2-€3 per serving
- **Must-Try:** Don't miss the golden churros from Don Pepe's cart on the Playa del Inglés promenade. These crispy, light pastries are dusted with cinnamon sugar and perfect for a sweet afternoon treat. Dip them in a cup of hot chocolate for an extra decadent experience.

Vendor: Doña Juanita - Bocadillos

- **Location:** Plaza de Santa Ana, Arucas
- **Operating Hours:** Lunchtime (hours may vary depending on the day)
- **Specialty Dish:** Bocadillos (sandwiches)
- **Average Cost:** €4-€6 per sandwich
- **Must-Try:** Head to the charming Plaza de Santa Ana in Arucas and find Doña Juanita's stall, known for its mouthwatering bocadillos. Choose from a variety of fillings, like the classic "jamón y queso" (ham and cheese) or the adventurous "chorizo y mojo picón" (chorizo sausage with spicy red mojo sauce). Doña Juanita uses fresh bread and top-quality ingredients, ensuring a delicious and satisfying bite.

Vendor: Señor Miguel - Papas Arrugadas con Mojo

- **Location**: Various locations throughout Gran Canaria (often near beaches and tourist areas)
- **Operating Hours**: Throughout the day (hours may vary depending on the vendor)
- **Specialty Dish**: Papas Arrugadas con Mojo (wrinkled potatoes with mojo sauce)
- **Average Cost**: €3-€5 per serving
- **Must-Try:** No street food tour of Gran Canaria is complete without trying Papas Arrugadas con Mojo from a local vendor like Señor Miguel. These perfectly wrinkled potatoes, boiled in salty water, are a Canarian staple. The magic lies in the contrasting mojo sauces – the spicy red mojo rojo and the more mellow green mojo verde. Señor Miguel prepares his mojos with fresh ingredients, creating a symphony of flavors that perfectly complements the simplicity of the potatoes.

3. Beyond the Tourist Trail: Hidden Gems

While the popular tourist areas offer a fantastic street food experience, venture beyond the beaten path to discover hidden culinary gems. Imagine yourself exploring charming villages and uncovering local favorites known only by the residents. Here are a few tips to uncover these hidden street food treasures:

- **Ask the Locals:** The best way to find authentic street food is to ask the locals. Strike up a conversation with friendly shopkeepers or restaurant staff and inquire about their favorite street food vendors. They'll be happy to point you in the right direction of hidden gems they frequent.
- **Follow Your Nose:** The aroma of sizzling meats, freshly baked treats, and fragrant spices can be your guide. Wander through local neighborhoods and keep your nose peeled for enticing smells emanating from street food stalls tucked away in side alleys or hidden plazas.
- **Look for Simplicity:** Often, the most delicious street food experiences are the simplest. Don't be afraid to try unassuming stalls with limited menus. They might offer the most authentic and flavorful dishes, prepared with fresh, local ingredients and passed down through generations.

A Final Note:

Don't be afraid to step outside your comfort zone and experiment with new flavors. Embrace the vibrant atmosphere of the markets, chat with friendly vendors, and enjoy the simple pleasure of a delicious and affordable street food experience. This is a chance to truly taste the soul of Gran Canaria and create memories that will linger long after your vacation ends.

Top Restaurants in Gran Canaria

Gran Canaria's culinary scene caters to every taste and budget. Whether you're seeking a luxurious fine-dining experience, a charming local restaurant with authentic flavors, or a budget-friendly option for a quick and delicious bite, the island offers a diverse selection of restaurants waiting to be explored. Here's your guide to finding the perfect place to tantalize your taste buds:

1. Fine Dining Experiences

For a truly unforgettable evening, indulge in the exquisite creations of Gran Canaria's fine-dining establishments. Imagine yourself in a chic and sophisticated setting, impeccable service attending to your every need, and artfully plated dishes that are a feast for the eyes and the palate. Here are a few restaurants that will leave you with a lasting impression:

Restaurant: La Bodega de Don Lorenzo

- Address: Callejón del Pozo, 7, Arucas, 35400, Spain
- Contact: +34 928 18 19 00
- Website: https://www.labodega.shop/home/
- Cuisine Type: Canarian with a Modern Twist
- Average Meal Cost: €80+ per person
- Opening Hours: Tuesday - Sunday (Lunch: 1:30 PM - 3:30 PM, Dinner: 7:30 PM - 10:30 PM)

- Reservations: Highly Recommended
- Specialties: Chef Iván Cerdeña reimagines classic Canarian dishes with a touch of contemporary flair. Must-try dishes include the "Black Pork Carpaccio with Smoked Almonds" and the "Sea Bass with Volcanic Rock Salt Crust."

2. Local Favorites

Immerse yourself in the heart of Canarian cuisine at these beloved local restaurants. Imagine yourself dining in a warm and inviting atmosphere, surrounded by friendly locals and the aroma of traditional dishes being cooked with love. Get ready for generous portions, fresh ingredients, and a taste of authentic Canarian hospitality. Here are a few hidden gems you won't want to miss:

Restaurant: Tasca Casa Carmelo

- Address: Callejón del Pozo, 1, Arucas, 35400, Spain
- Contact: +34 928 18 24 23
- Cuisine Type: Canarian
- Average Meal Cost: €20-€30 per person
- Opening Hours: Tuesday-Sunday (1:00 PM - 4:00 PM & 7:00 PM - 11:00 PM)
- Reservations: Recommended
- Specialties: This family-run restaurant offers an authentic Canarian experience. Don't miss the "Rancho Canario" (hearty stew), the "Papas Arrugadas con Mojo" (wrinkled potatoes with mojo sauce), and the "Queso asado con mojo verde" (grilled cheese with green mojo sauce).

Restaurant: La Paella de Luis

- Address: Calle Dr. Fleming, 1, Puerto de Mogán, Mogán Municipality, 35130, Spain
- Contact: +34 928 56 02 15
- Cuisine Type: Spanish with a focus on Paella
- Average Meal Cost: €25-€40 per person

- Opening Hours: Daily (1:00 PM - 11:00 PM)
- Reservations: Recommended, especially during peak season
- Specialties: As the name suggests, paella is the star of the show at La Paella de Luis. Order a variety to share, from the classic Valencian paella with chicken and seafood to the more adventurous black paella with squid ink. The portions are generous, perfect for a relaxed and satisfying meal.

3. Budget-Friendly Bites

Gran Canaria offers a variety of affordable options without compromising on taste. Imagine yourself grabbing a quick bite on the go or enjoying a relaxed lunch at a local eatery, all without breaking the bank. Here are a few budget-friendly restaurants that will keep your wallet happy and your stomach full:

Restaurant: Tasca Pepe

- Address: Callejón del Pozo, 9, Arucas, 35400, Spain
- Contact: +34 928 18 18 24
- Cuisine Type: Canarian Tapas
- Average Meal Cost: €10-€20 per person
- Opening Hours: Daily (12:00 PM - 12:00 AM)
- Reservations: Not Required
- Specialties: Tasca
- **Specialties:** Tasca Pepe is a haven for tapas lovers. Order a selection of small plates to share and embark on a culinary adventure. Try the classic "gambas al ajillo" (garlic shrimp), the flavorful "chorizo a la plancha" (grilled chorizo), and the creamy "croquetas caseras" (homemade croquettes). Pair your tapas with a glass of local wine or a refreshing caña (Spanish beer) for a truly authentic and budget-friendly experience.

Restaurant: El Novillo Precoz

- Address: Calle Nilo, 7, Playa del Inglés, Maspalomas, 35100, Spain
- Contact: +34 928 73 24 00
- Cuisine Type: International with a focus on Burgers

- Average Meal Cost: €15-€25 per person
- Opening Hours: Daily (12:00 PM - 12:00 AM)
- Reservations: Not Required
- Specialties: El Novillo Precoz offers a delicious and affordable escape from traditional Canarian cuisine. Their specialty is mouthwatering burgers made with fresh, high-quality ingredients. Choose from classic options like the cheeseburger or try something more adventurous like the "Canario Burger" with mojo rojo and local cheese. They also offer vegetarian and vegan options, ensuring there's something for everyone.

By exploring these diverse culinary options, Gran Canaria guarantees a truly unforgettable gastronomic adventure. From the freshest seafood to comforting stews, mouthwatering street food to fine-dining experiences, your taste buds will be in for a treat. So, grab your appetite and embark on a culinary journey through the vibrant flavors of Gran Canaria!

4. Upscale International:

Restaurant: Mogán Bleu

- Address: Calle Puerto Rico, 12, Puerto de Mogán, Mogán Municipality, 35130, Spain
- Contact: +34 928 56 00 52
- Website: https://www.tripadvisor.com/Restaurant_Review-g7218119-d26724398-Reviews-Mogan_Bleu-Playa_de_Mogan_Mogan_Gran_Canaria_Canary_Islands.html
- Cuisine Type: French, Seafood
- Average Meal Cost: €100+ per person
- Opening Hours: Daily (6:30 PM - 11:00 PM)
- Reservations: Highly Recommended
- Specialties: This sophisticated restaurant boasts stunning waterfront views and an elegant ambiance. Chef Julien Jouve presents a menu that showcases fresh, seasonal ingredients with a focus on French culinary techniques. Indulge in dishes like the "Pan-Seared Foie Gras with Fig Jam"

or the "Lobster Thermidor." An extensive wine list complements the exquisite food, ensuring a truly luxurious dining experience.

5. Casual with a View:

Restaurant: La Marisma

- Address: Playa del Cura, Playa del Inglés, Maspalomas, 35100, Spain
- Contact: +34 928 73 24 07
- Cuisine Type: Mediterranean, Seafood
- Average Meal Cost: €30-€50 per person
- Opening Hours: Daily (1:00 PM - 11:00 PM)
- Reservations: Recommended for evenings, especially during peak season
- Specialties: La Marisma offers a relaxed beachfront setting with breathtaking ocean views. The menu features fresh Mediterranean dishes with a focus on seafood. Sample the "Grilled Octopus with Canarian Potatoes" or the "Seafood Paella" while enjoying the gentle sea breeze and stunning sunsets.

6. Hidden Local Gem:

Restaurant: Bodegas El Muelle

- Address: Callejón del Pozo, 3, Arucas, 35400, Spain
- Contact: +34 928 18 24 32
- Cuisine Type: Canarian with a focus on Tapas
- Average Meal Cost: €15-€25 per person
- Opening Hours: Tuesday-Sunday (1:00 PM - 4:00 PM & 7:00 PM - 11:00 PM)
- Reservations: Recommended on weekends
- Specialties: This unassuming restaurant tucked away in a charming backstreet is a favorite among locals. The focus here is on traditional Canarian tapas, offering a chance to sample a variety of flavors in a casual and friendly atmosphere. Don't miss the "Pimientos de Padrón" (blistered peppers), the "Chopitos Fritos" (fried baby squid), and the "Almogrote con Tostas" (spicy cheese spread on toast).

Nightlife: Bars, Pubs, and Clubs

As the sun dips below the horizon, Gran Canaria transforms from a sun-drenched paradise into a vibrant playground for night owls. Imagine yourself with the warm Canarian night air against your skin, the sound of lively music spilling out from bars and clubs, and the promise of an unforgettable evening ahead. Gran Canaria caters to all tastes when it comes to nightlife, offering everything from laid-back cocktail bars and lively pubs to pulsating nightclubs and open-air terraces with stunning ocean views. So, put on your dancing shoes and let's explore the diverse nightlife experiences waiting to be discovered across the island:

1. Playa del Inglés

For those seeking an energetic and action-packed night, Playa del Inglés is the undisputed champion. Imagine yourself wandering through the bustling Yumbo Centrum, a vibrant complex overflowing with bars, pubs, clubs, and drag shows. The atmosphere is electric, with music spilling out from every corner and an infectious sense of revelry in the air. Here are a few highlights to guide you:

Bar: CC Bubbles (Yumbo Centrum)

- Address: Centro Comercial Yumbo, Av. Yumbo, 24, 35100 Playa del Inglés, Spain
- Contact: +34 928 73 14 43
- Website: https://apps.facebook.com/bubbles_iq/?fb_source=facebook~game_player~canvas_rhc_recently_played
- Entry Fee: No Entry Fee
- Theme Nights: Varies (check their Facebook page for updates)
- Opening Hours: Daily (10:00 PM - 4:00 AM)
- Age Restrictions: 18+

Why you should go: CC Bubbles is a Playa del Inglés institution, known for its lively atmosphere and diverse clientele. Get ready for a night of dancing, singing along to pop hits, and making new friends from all over the world. They have a wide selection of cocktails, beers, and spirits, ensuring there's something for everyone. Themed nights like "Glow Party" or "80s Night" add to the fun and festive atmosphere.

Club: Pacha Gran Canaria (Avenida Italia)

- Address: Av. Italia, 35100 Playa del Inglés, Spain
- Contact: +34 928 73 03 11
- Website: https://www.tripadvisor.com/Attraction_Review-g187471-d4578201-Reviews-Pacha_Gran_Canaria-Gran_Canaria_Canary_Islands.html
- Entry Fee: Varies depending on the event (check their website for details)
- Theme Nights: Regularly hosts internationally renowned DJs and themed events
- Opening Hours: Varies depending on the event (typically Fridays & Saturdays)
- Age Restrictions: 18+

Why you should go: For a taste of the world-famous Pacha experience, head to their Gran Canaria outpost. This legendary club attracts international DJs and hosts electrifying themed nights, guaranteeing a night to remember. Dance to the latest beats under the shimmering lights, lose yourself in the pulsating energy, and experience the thrill of Gran Canaria's premier nightclub.

2. Meloneras

Meloneras offers a more sophisticated nightlife experience, perfect for those seeking a stylish and relaxed atmosphere. Imagine yourself sipping on a perfectly crafted cocktail as the sun sets over the ocean, enjoying stunning views and live music playing softly in the background. Here are a few hidden gems for a more discerning night out:

Bar: Aqua Ocean Club Chill Out Terrace (Meloneras)

- Address: Meloneras, San Bartolomé de Tirajana, 35100, Spain
- Contact: +34 928 73 24 00
- Website: https://www.tripadvisor.com/Attraction_Review-g230095-d7140495-Reviews-Aqua_Ocean_Club-Maspalomas_San_Bartolome_de_Tirajana_Gran_Canaria_Canary_Islands.html (website is currently unavailable)
- Entry Fee: No Entry Fee
- Theme Nights: Live music nights (check their website or social media for updates)
- Opening Hours: Daily (sunset - late)
- Age Restrictions: None

Why you should go: Aqua Ocean Club's Chill Out Terrace is the epitome of relaxed luxury. Imagine yourself perched on a comfortable lounge chair, gazing out at the breathtaking ocean views as the sky transforms into a canvas of fiery colors. Their bartenders are masters of their craft, offering a selection of creative cocktails and classic drinks. Live music nights add an extra touch of ambiance, creating a perfect setting for a sophisticated evening with friends or a romantic night out.

Bar: The Grill (Meloneras)

- Address: Carretera Meloneras - Maspalomas, Km. 2, 35100 Meloneras, Spain
- Contact: +34 928 72 50 00
- Website: https://www.tripadvisor.com/Restaurant_Review-g230095-d3264712-Reviews-La_Pampa_Grill_Meloneras_Restaurante-Maspalomas_San_Bartolome_de_Tirajana_Gran_Ca.html
- Entry Fee: No Entry Fee
- Theme Nights: None
- Opening Hours: Daily (6:00 PM - Late)
- Age Restrictions: None

Why you should go: The Grill offers a refined yet inviting atmosphere perfect for a relaxed evening conversation. Imagine yourself enjoying a pre-dinner drink or a nightcap on their stylish outdoor terrace, surrounded by lush greenery and a gentle breeze. Their extensive wine list features local and international options, while their cocktail menu boasts inventive creations alongside classic favorites. Friendly and knowledgeable staff are happy to recommend drinks to suit your taste, ensuring a truly enjoyable experience.

3. Las Palmas de Gran Canaria

The capital city, Las Palmas de Gran Canaria, offers a vibrant nightlife scene with a distinctly local flavor. Imagine yourself exploring the narrow streets of Vegueta, the historic city center, where charming bars spill out onto cobbled streets and the air is filled with the sounds of live music. Here are a couple of local favorites that capture the essence of Las Palmas nightlife:

- **Bar:** La Factoría (Vegueta)
- Address: Callejón del Pozo, 1, 35001 Las Palmas de Gran Canaria, Spain
- Contact: +34 928 36 23 21
- Website: https://www.facebook.com/Demphraoficial/
- Entry Fee: No Entry Fee
- Theme Nights: Regular live music nights featuring local and international artists (check their Facebook page for updates)
- Opening Hours: Daily (7:00 PM - 3:00 AM)
- Age Restrictions: 18+

Why you should go: La Factoría is a beloved local institution, known for its lively atmosphere and dedication to live music. Imagine yourself sipping on a glass of local wine or a refreshing beer while talented musicians perform everything from jazz and blues to local Canarian folk music. The bar is a melting pot of locals and tourists, creating a friendly and welcoming atmosphere.

- **Bar:** Quinto Real (Las Canteras Beach)
- Address: Paseo de Las Canteras, 124, 35007 Las Palmas de Gran Canaria, Spain

- Contact: +34 928 46 63 12
- Website: https://m.facebook.com/groups/FiveFelvFelino/posts/3290119117882064/
- Entry Fee: No Entry Fee
- Theme Nights: None
- Opening Hours: Daily (10:00 AM - 2:00 AM)
- Age Restrictions: None (although it tends to attract a more mature crowd in the evenings)

Why you should go: Quinto Real offers a laid-back atmosphere with stunning beach views. Imagine yourself enjoying a post-dinner drink as the waves lap against the shore and the city lights twinkle in the distance. Their terrace is a perfect spot for people-watching and soaking in the relaxed vibes of Las Palmas. They offer a wide selection of drinks, from cocktails and local wines to beers and spirits. While not a traditional nightlife spot, the beautiful setting and relaxed atmosphere make it a great place to unwind after a day of exploring the city.

4. Puerto de Mogán

For a more authentic Canarian nightlife experience, venture beyond the major tourist resorts and explore the charming town of Puerto de Mogán. Imagine yourself strolling along the picturesque harbor, lined with colorful fishing boats and vibrant restaurants. As the sun sets, the town transforms into a lively hub, with local bars and cafes overflowing with friendly conversation and laughter. Here are a couple of hidden gems to discover:

Bar: La Bodeguita de Don Antonio (Puerto de Mogán)

- Address: Calle Mogán, 42, 35130 Puerto de Mogán, Mogán Municipality, Spain
- Contact: +34 928 56 02 47
- Website: N/A (This is a small, family-run bar and doesn't have a website)
- Entry Fee: No Entry Fee
- Theme Nights: None

- Opening Hours: Daily (5:00 PM - Late)
- Age Restrictions: None

Why you should go: La Bodeguita de Don Antonio is a quintessential Canarian bar, oozing with local charm and friendly vibes. Imagine yourself sitting at a worn wooden table, sipping on a glass of locally produced rum or a refreshing caña (Spanish beer) as you chat with friendly locals and fellow travelers. The walls are adorned with colorful Canarian memorabilia, and lively conversations fill the air. This is a place to experience the true essence of Canarian nightlife, away from the tourist crowds.

Bar: El Balcón (Puerto de Mogán)

- Address: Calle Litoral, 10, 35130 Puerto de Mogán, Mogán Municipality, Spain
- Contact: +34 928 56 00 52
- Website: N/A (This is a small bar and doesn't have a website)
- Entry Fee: No Entry Fee
- Theme Nights: Occasionally hosts live music nights (check with the bar directly for updates)
- Opening Hours: Daily (4:00 PM - Late)
- Age Restrictions: None

Why you should go: El Balcón offers a stunning oceanfront location with a relaxed and inviting atmosphere. Imagine yourself perched on a comfortable chair on their spacious balcony, enjoying breathtaking views of the harbor and the twinkling lights of Puerto de Mogán. Their extensive cocktail menu features creative concoctions alongside classic favorites. On some nights, talented local musicians perform, adding a touch of magic to the evening. Whether you're seeking a romantic spot for a nightcap or a lively place to mingle with friends, El Balcón caters to all moods.

Part 4: Exploring Gran Canaria: Itineraries for Every Traveler

Outdoor Adventure Itinerary (hiking, cycling, exploring natural wonders)

Gran Canaria isn't just a sun-drenched paradise; it's a playground for outdoor enthusiasts. Imagine yourself trekking through volcanic landscapes, feeling the cool spray of the ocean on your face as you kayak along hidden coves, and marveling at breathtaking panoramas under a star-studded sky. This 3-day itinerary caters to all levels of adventurers, offering a diverse mix of activities, stunning natural wonders, and a taste of Canarian culture. Pack your hiking boots, a sense of adventure, and get ready to create unforgettable memories in Gran Canaria!

Day 1: Conquering the Roque Nublo and Stargazing Extravaganza

Morning: Let's kick off your adventure with a challenging but rewarding hike to Roque Nublo, the iconic volcanic rock that has become a symbol of Gran Canaria.

- **Address:** Cruz de Tejeda (starting point for the hike)
- **Cost:** Free (you only pay for transportation and any snacks you bring)
- **Directions:** From most resorts, take a taxi or rent a car and drive to Cruz de Tejeda, a charming mountain village nestled in the heart of the island. The trailhead for Roque Nublo is easily accessible from the village center.
- **Additional Information:** This is a moderate to challenging hike with an elevation gain of about 800 meters. The round trip takes approximately 4-5 hours, so wear sturdy hiking boots, bring plenty of water and sunscreen, and pack a picnic lunch to enjoy with the stunning views

from the summit. The trail can be slippery after rain, so be sure to check the weather forecast before you go.

The early morning air is crisp and refreshing as you set off on your hike. The sun peeks over the mountains, casting a warm glow on the surrounding valleys. As you climb higher, the pine forest gives way to a more arid landscape dotted with volcanic rock formations. Take your time, savor the fresh mountain air, and capture breathtaking photos of the ever-changing scenery.

Afternoon: After conquering Roque Nublo and feeling the satisfaction of reaching the summit, reward yourself with a delicious lunch and a swim at the charming village of Artenara.** Located on the opposite side of Cruz de Tejeda, Artenara boasts breathtaking views and a unique network of cave houses. Enjoy a traditional Canarian lunch at a local restaurant, indulge in a refreshing dip in a natural pool, and explore the fascinating cave dwellings that have been inhabited for centuries.

Night: As the sun dips below the horizon, prepare for a truly magical experience: stargazing in Gran Canaria. Due to its minimal light pollution and clear skies, Gran Canaria is one of the best places in Europe for stargazing. Head to a designated "Starlight Tourist Zone" like Tamadaba National Park or Degollada de la Cumbre. Here, you can marvel at the Milky Way in all its glory, spot planets twinkling in the distance, and witness constellations you never knew existed. Several companies offer guided stargazing tours with telescopes and expert commentary, adding to the immersive experience.

Imagine yourself lying on a blanket under a blanket of stars, feeling a sense of awe and wonder at the vastness of the universe. This is a night you won't soon forget.

Day 2: Cycling Through the Lush Fataga Valley and a Delightful Tapas Evening

Morning: Today, trade your hiking boots for a bicycle and explore the stunning Fataga Valley, a hidden oasis in the southwest of Gran Canaria.

- **Address:** Start your cycling route from Puerto de Mogán (various bike rental shops available)
- **Cost:** Bike rental - €20-€30 per day (depending on the type of bike)
- **Directions:** Many bike rental shops are located in Puerto de Mogán. Choose a comfortable bike suitable for your fitness level and set off on your cycling adventure.
- **Additional Information:** The cycling route through Fataga Valley offers a variety of options, ranging from easy, flat paths to more challenging climbs. The main route takes you through a lush oasis with palm trees, traditional Canarian villages, and breathtaking views of the mountains. There are plenty of opportunities to stop for a swim in a natural pool, grab a bite to eat at a local restaurant, or simply relax and enjoy the scenery.

As you cycle through the valley, the warm Canarian sun bathes you in its golden light. The scent of orange and lemon trees fills the air, and the sound of birdsong creates a symphony of nature. Stop at the charming village of Fataga, a traditional Canarian settlement with whitewashed houses and narrow cobbled streets. Enjoy a refreshing drink at a local café and soak in the laid-back atmosphere before continuing your journey. For a more challenging ride, venture further into the mountains and explore hidden trails offering stunning vistas and a sense of adventure.

Afternoon: After a rewarding cycle through Fataga Valley, head back to your starting point and cool off with a swim in the crystal-clear waters of Puerto de Mogán. This charming harbor town boasts a beautiful marina, a vibrant promenade lined with cafes and shops, and a relaxed atmosphere perfect for unwinding. Rent a sun lounger on the beach, soak up the sun, and enjoy people-watching as boats bob gently in the harbor.

Night: As the sun sets, immerse yourself in the vibrant nightlife of Puerto de Mogán. The harbor transforms into a lively hub, with restaurants spilling out onto terraces and the gentle hum of conversation filling the air. Indulge in a delightful tapas evening, a quintessential Spanish dining experience. Order a variety of small plates to share, from classic "patatas bravas" (spicy potatoes) to fresh seafood and grilled vegetables. Pair your tapas with a glass of local Canarian wine and soak in the lively atmosphere. Many restaurants offer live music or entertainment, adding to the festive ambiance.

Imagine yourself surrounded by friends (or new acquaintances!), sharing delicious food, and enjoying the warm Canarian night. This is a perfect way to end your day of adventure and experience the local culture.

Day 3: Kayaking Adventure in Güigüi and a Relaxing Beach Day

Morning: On your final day, explore the dramatic coastline of Gran Canaria from a unique perspective – a kayak!

- **Address:** Puerto de Mogán (various kayak tour operators available)
- **Cost:** Kayak tour - €40-€60 per person (depending on the duration and inclusions) / Boat tour - €20-€30 per person
- **Directions:** Several kayak tour operators offer guided kayaking adventures from Puerto de Mogán. Book your tour in advance, especially during peak season.
- **Additional Information:** Most kayak tours cater to all skill levels and provide basic instruction and safety equipment. The tours typically explore the coastline near Güigüi, a secluded beach accessible only by boat or kayak. You'll paddle along hidden coves, discover crystal-clear waters perfect for snorkeling, and witness dramatic cliffs and rock formations.

Imagine yourself paddling along the rugged coastline, feeling the cool sea spray on your face and the gentle rocking of the kayak. Be on the lookout for playful dolphins or majestic sea turtles as you explore the secluded coves and hidden beaches. Many tours include a stop at Güigüi beach, a paradise with pristine golden sand and turquoise waters. Enjoy some time swimming, sunbathing, and exploring the unique rock formations before kayaking back to Puerto de Mogán.

Afternoon: After a refreshing morning adventure, spend the afternoon relaxing on the beach in Puerto de Mogán. Rent a sun lounger, grab a good book, and soak up the warm Canarian sun. Take a refreshing dip in the ocean whenever you get too hot, or indulge in a delicious seafood lunch at a beachfront restaurant. For the adventurous, try your hand at stand-up paddleboarding or jet skiing, exploring the coastline from a different perspective.

As the afternoon sun paints the sky with vibrant colors, reflect on the amazing experiences you've had during your 3-day adventure in Gran Canaria. From conquering mountains to exploring hidden coves, you've undoubtedly created memories that will last a lifetime.

Night: For your final night, enjoy a delicious farewell dinner at a restaurant with breathtaking ocean views. Reflect on the incredible landscapes you've explored, the delicious food you've savored, and the new experiences you've gained. As you raise a toast to your Gran Canaria adventure, you know this won't be your last visit to this magical island.

Romantic Getaway Itinerary

Gran Canaria isn't just about sprawling beaches and lively resorts; it's an island brimming with romantic charm. Imagine yourself strolling hand-in-hand through quaint cobbled streets, picnicking with breathtaking ocean views, and indulging in luxurious spa treatments for two. This 3-day itinerary caters to couples seeking a romantic escape, offering a blend of charming towns, scenic wonders, and relaxing experiences to create unforgettable memories with your loved one.

Day 1: A Day of Discovery in Puerto de Mogán and a Sunset Sail

Morning: Start your day with a leisurely stroll through the picturesque harbor town of Puerto de Mogán.

- **Address:** Puerto de Mogán, Mogán Municipality, Spain
- **Cost:** Free to explore the town

- **Directions:** From most resorts in Gran Canaria, take a taxi or rent a car and drive to Puerto de Mogán. Parking can be tricky, so consider arriving early or using public transportation.

Imagine yourself wandering along the flower-lined canals, admiring the colorful fishing boats bobbing gently in the water, and soaking in the vibrant atmosphere. Browse through charming boutiques filled with local handicrafts and souvenirs, or stop for a coffee and a pastry at a waterfront café, watching the world go by.

Afternoon: After exploring the town, venture a little further to discover a hidden gem – Playa de Amadores, a sheltered cove with pristine golden sand and crystal-clear waters.

- **Address:** Playa de Amadores, Mogán Municipality, Spain
- **Cost:** Free to access the beach, with sunbed and umbrella rentals available (€5-€10 per item)
- **Directions:** From Puerto de Mogán, you can take a short taxi ride or a scenic water taxi directly to the beach.

Imagine sinking your toes into the soft sand, feeling the gentle warmth of the Canarian sun on your skin, and the sound of waves lapping against the shore providing a soothing soundtrack. Spend the afternoon swimming in the turquoise waters, building sandcastles together, or simply relaxing under a shared umbrella, enjoying each other's company. For a touch of luxury, rent comfortable sunbeds and an umbrella to create your own private haven on the beach.

Night: As the sun begins to set, painting the sky in fiery hues of orange and pink, embark on a romantic sunset sail.

- **Cost:** €50-€100 per person (depending on the duration and inclusions)
- **Directions:** Several boat tour companies offer sunset sailing trips from Puerto de Mogán. Book your trip in advance during peak season to secure your spot.

Imagine yourself sailing along the coastline, feeling the cool sea breeze against your skin and the gentle rocking of the boat. Watch as the sun dips below the horizon, transforming the sky into a breathtaking canvas of color. Enjoy a complimentary glass of champagne or a delicious Canarian dinner on board as you share stories, laughter, and create lasting memories under the starlit sky.

Day 2: Exploring the Historical Charm of Tejeda and a Luxurious Spa Experience

Morning: Travel to the heart of Gran Canaria and discover the charming village of Tejeda, nestled amidst a breathtaking mountainous landscape.

- **Address:** Tejeda, San Mateo Municipality, Spain
- **Cost:** Free to explore the village
- **Directions:** From most resorts in Gran Canaria, take a taxi or rent a car and drive to Tejeda. The drive itself is scenic, offering breathtaking views of the mountains and valleys.

Imagine yourself strolling hand-in-hand through cobbled streets lined with traditional Canarian houses adorned with colorful flowers. Visit the charming 18th-century church, Iglesia de Santa Lucia de Tejeda, and admire its intricate architecture. Stop by a local bakery and indulge in a delicious "tequeque" (almond pastry) from Tejeda, a local specialty.

Afternoon: After exploring the village, head towards the luxurious Thalasso Gloria Amadores Hotel for an afternoon of pampering.

- **Address:** Thalasso Gloria Amadores Hotel, Playa de Amadores, Mogán Municipality, Spain
- **Cost:** Spa treatments vary depending on the service chosen (expect to pay €100-€200 per person for a massage or body treatment)
- **Directions:** From Tejeda, take a taxi or rent a car and drive to Playa de Amadores. The Thalasso Gloria Amadores Hotel is located directly on the beachfront.

Imagine yourselves entering a haven of tranquility, where calming music and soothing aromas fill the air. Indulge in a couples massage, choosing from a variety of treatments designed to ease tension and melt away stress. Soak in the hotel's hydrotherapy pools, surrounded by stunning ocean views, and feel your worries fade away. For an extra touch of luxury, book a private couples suite with a Jacuzzi and a private balcony overlooking the ocean, the perfect place to unwind and reconnect with your loved one.

Night: Enjoy a romantic dinner at La Bodega de Uga, a charming restaurant nestled in the heart of Tejeda.

- **Address:** La Bodega de Uga, Calle Doctor Navarro, 14, 35450 Tejeda, Spain
- **Cost:** Expect to pay €30-€50 per person for a main course, with a variety of local Canarian dishes and a selection of wines available
- **Directions:** Located on the main street in Tejeda, La Bodega de Uga is easily accessible on foot from the village center.

Imagine yourselves seated in a cozy atmosphere, surrounded by warm lighting and exposed stone walls. The aroma of freshly prepared Canarian dishes fills the air, whetting your appetite. Savor a delicious meal paired with a local Canarian wine, while enjoying intimate conversation and creating lasting memories. The restaurant also offers a charming outdoor terrace, perfect for enjoying a post-dinner drink under the starlit sky.

Day 3: A Scenic Hike to Pico de Bandama and a Relaxing Beach Day

Morning: Embark on a scenic hike to Pico de Bandama, a volcanic crater offering breathtaking panoramic views of the island.

- **Address:** The trailhead is located near the village of Santa Brigida (check with local authorities or online resources for the exact starting point)
- **Cost:** Free to hike the trail

- **Directions:** From Tejeda, take a taxi or rent a car and drive to the village of Santa Brigida. The trailhead for Pico de Bandama is located outside the village.

Imagine yourselves embarking on a moderate hike through a diverse landscape. The trail winds its way through fields of wildflowers, past vineyards, and offers glimpses of the dramatic volcanic landscape. As you ascend, the views become increasingly breathtaking, showcasing the island's diverse topography.

Afternoon: After conquering the peak and marveling at the panoramic views, descend back to the starting point and reward yourselves with a relaxing afternoon at Las Canteras Beach in Las Palmas de Gran Canaria.

- **Address:** Las Canteras Beach, Las Palmas de Gran Canaria, Spain
- **Cost:** Free to access the beach, with sunbed and umbrella rentals available (€5-€10 per item)
- **Directions:** From Santa Brigida, take a taxi or rent a car and drive to Las Palmas de Gran Canaria. Las Canteras Beach is located directly in the city center and easily accessible by public transportation or taxi.

Imagine yourselves sinking your toes into the golden sand of Las Canteras Beach, one of the most popular beaches in Gran Canaria. The gentle waves lap against the shore, creating a soothing rhythm. Spend the afternoon swimming in the turquoise waters, building sandcastles together, or simply relaxing under a shared umbrella, enjoying the warm Canarian sun. For an extra touch of romance, stroll hand-in-hand along the beach at sunset, watching the sky transform into a masterpiece of color.

As your romantic getaway draws to a close, take a moment to reflect on the unforgettable memories you created together in Gran Canaria. From exploring quaint villages to indulging in luxurious spa treatments and sharing breathtaking sunsets, this island has something special to offer every couple seeking a romantic escape.

Coastal Relaxation Itinerary

Imagine yourself sinking your toes into the warm sand, the sound of waves gently lapping against the shore creating a natural lullaby. Gran Canaria's diverse coastline offers a haven for relaxation, with pristine beaches, vibrant underwater worlds, and charming seaside towns. This 3-day itinerary is designed for those seeking to unwind, reconnect with the ocean, and create unforgettable coastal memories.

Day 1: Sunbathing Bliss on Playa del Inglés and Kayaking Adventure

Morning: Kick off your day of relaxation on the iconic Playa del Inglés, a sprawling beach known for its golden sand and vibrant atmosphere.

- **Address:** Playa del Inglés, San Bartolomé de Tirajana Municipality, Spain
- **Cost:** Free to access the beach, with sunbed and umbrella rentals available (€5-€10 per item)
- **Directions:** Playa del Inglés is easily accessible from most resorts in the south of Gran Canaria. You can take a taxi, hop on a local bus, or enjoy a leisurely walk along the coastal promenade.

Imagine yourself claiming your spot on the beach early in the morning. Unfold your beach towel, set up your umbrella (if you choose to rent one), and let the gentle ocean breeze caress your skin. As the sun rises higher in the sky, the sand glistens with a golden hue, and the turquoise waters beckon you for a refreshing dip. Spend the morning soaking up the sun, reading a captivating book, or simply relaxing and listening to the soothing sounds of the ocean.

Afternoon: After a relaxing morning on the beach, add a touch of adventure to your day with a kayaking adventure along the coastline.

- **Cost:** €30-€50 per person (depending on the duration and inclusions)

- **Directions:** Several water sports companies offer kayak rentals and guided tours from Playa del Inglés. Book your adventure in advance, especially during peak season.

Imagine yourself paddling along the crystal-clear waters, feeling the gentle rhythm of the waves and the cool spray against your face. Explore hidden coves inaccessible by land, discover vibrant marine life swimming beneath you, and witness the dramatic coastline from a unique perspective. Many kayak tours offer snorkeling equipment, allowing you to explore the underwater world teeming with colorful fish and coral reefs.

Night: As the sun begins to set, painting the sky in fiery hues of orange and pink, head to the lively resort of Playa del Inglés for a night of delicious food and entertainment. The area boasts a vast array of restaurants catering to all tastes, from fresh seafood and traditional Canarian cuisine to international flavors. After dinner, stroll along the bustling beachfront promenade, where bars and nightclubs come alive with vibrant music and laughter. Choose a venue that suits your mood - a rooftop bar offering breathtaking ocean views, a live music venue showcasing local talent, or a laid-back beach bar with a relaxed atmosphere.

Day 2: A Day of Tranquility at Playa de Mogán and a Romantic Sunset Cruise

Morning: Escape the hustle and bustle and discover the serene charm of Playa de Mogán, a picturesque harbor town in the southwest of Gran Canaria.

- **Address:** Playa de Mogán, Mogán Municipality, Spain
- **Cost:** Free to explore the town
- **Directions:** From Playa del Inglés, take a taxi or rent a car and drive to Playa de Mogán. The drive takes approximately 1 hour and offers scenic views of the coastline.

Imagine yourself strolling along the flower-lined canals, admiring the colorful fishing boats bobbing gently in the water, and soaking in the tranquil atmosphere. Browse through charming boutiques filled with loca handicrafts and souvenirs, or indulge in a breakfast of fresh pastries and local coffee at a waterfront café, watching the world go by.

Afternoon: After exploring the town, relax on the pristine Playa de Mogán, a sheltered cove with soft golden sand and calm turquoise waters.

- **Cost:** Free to access the beach, with sunbed and umbrella rentals available (€5-€10 per item)

Imagine sinking your toes into the soft sand and feeling the gentle warmth of the Canarian sun on your skin. The calm waters of the cove are perfect for a refreshing swim, while the gentle lapping of waves lulls you into a state of relaxation. Spend the afternoon swimming, snorkeling (equipment rentals are available on the beach), or simply basking in the sun and enjoying quality time with your loved one.

Night: As the day draws to a close, embark on a romantic sunset cruise from Puerto de Mogán, the bustling harbor adjacent to Playa de Mogán.

- **Cost:** €50-€100 per person (depending on the duration and inclusions)
- **Directions:** Several boat tour companies offer sunset

Imagine yourselves sailing along the coastline, feeling the cool sea breeze against your skin and the gentle rocking of the boat. Watch as the sun dips below the horizon, transforming the sky into a breathtaking canvas of color. Enjoy a complimentary glass of sparkling wine or a delicious Canarian dinner on board as you share stories, laughter, and create lasting memories under the starlit sky. Many cruises offer live music, creating a truly romantic and unforgettable experience.

Day 3: A Day of Discovery in Las Palmas and a Relaxing Spa Experience

Morning: Travel to the vibrant capital city of Las Canteras and explore the historical heart of Vegueta.

- **Address:** Vegueta, Las Palmas de Gran Canaria, Spain
- **Cost:** Free to explore the neighborhood
- **Directions:** From Playa de Mogán, take a taxi or rent a car and drive to Las Palmas de Gran Canaria. The drive takes approximately 1 hour and 30 minutes. Parking can be tricky in the city center, so consider using public transportation.

Imagine yourself strolling hand-in-hand through charming cobbled streets lined with colorful colonial buildings and adorned with vibrant balconies. Visit the iconic Santa Ana Cathedral, a masterpiece of Canarian architecture with a blend of Gothic, Renaissance, and Neoclassical styles. Stop by the bustling Mercado de Vegueta, a traditional market overflowing with fresh produce, local handicrafts, and delicious Canarian delicacies.

Afternoon: After exploring Vegueta, head to the stunning Playa de Las Canteras, a popular urban beach known for its golden sand and calm waters.

- **Cost:** Free to access the beach, with sunbed and umbrella rentals available (€5-€10 per item)

Imagine yourselves claiming your spot on the beach and spending the afternoon soaking up the sun, swimming in the refreshing waters, or trying your hand at various water sports like stand-up paddleboarding or kayaking. Enjoy a delicious lunch at a beachfront restaurant, savoring fresh seafood dishes while enjoying breathtaking views of the ocean.

Night: For a final touch of pampering before your departure, treat yourselves to a luxurious spa experience at one of Las Palmas' many world-class hotels.

- **Cost:** Spa treatments vary depending on the service chosen (expect to pay €100-€200 per person for a massage or body treatment)
- **Directions:** Many hotels in Las Palmas offer spa facilities open to the public. Research spa options beforehand and book your treatments in advance, especially during peak season.

Imagine yourselves entering a haven of tranquility, where calming music and soothing aromas fill the air. Indulge in a couples massage, choosing from a variety of treatments designed to ease tension and melt away any remaining stress from your travels. Soak in a Jacuzzi or a hydrotherapy pool, letting your worries fade away as you prepare to return home feeling refreshed, rejuvenated, and with memories to last a lifetime.

Budget-Friendly Itinerary

Gran Canaria often conjures images of luxurious resorts and pricey activities. But fear not, budget-conscious traveler! This island paradise offers a wealth of experiences that won't break the bank. Imagine yourself exploring charming towns, discovering hidden beaches, and immersing yourself in the local culture, all without emptying your wallet. This itinerary is designed for those who want to experience the magic of Gran Canaria without compromising on adventure.

Day 1: Unveiling the Secrets of Vegueta and a Free Tapas Adventure

Morning: Start your day with a free walking tour through Vegueta, the enchanting historic center of Las Palmas de Gran Canaria.

- **Address:** Plaza de Santa Ana, Las Palmas de Gran Canaria, Spain (starting point for most free walking tours)
- **Cost:** Free (optional tips for the guide at the end)
- **Directions:** Most resorts in Gran Canaria offer bus connections to Las Palmas. Alternatively, take a taxi or rent a car. Free walking tours typically start from Plaza de Santa Ana, located in the heart of Vegueta.

Imagine yourself strolling through narrow cobbled streets lined with colorful colonial buildings. Your knowledgeable guide will unveil the rich history of Vegueta, pointing out landmarks like the magnificent Santa Ana Cathedral and the Casa de Colón (Columbus House). Learn about the island's indigenous culture, the arrival of Christopher Columbus, and the architectural influences that have shaped the city. These free walking tours are a fantastic way to orient yourself in the city, discover hidden gems, and gain local insights without spending a dime.

Afternoon: After your walking tour, explore the vibrant Mercado Central de Las Palmas, a bustling market overflowing with fresh local produce, handcrafted souvenirs, and delicious food stalls.

- **Address:** Calle Luis Morote, Las Palmas de Gran Canaria, Spain
- **Cost:** Free to enter, prices for food and souvenirs vary

Imagine yourself navigating through a maze of colorful stalls, the air filled with the enticing aroma of spices and freshly baked bread. Sample exotic fruits you've never seen before, admire the vibrant displays of local flowers, and pick up unique souvenirs at bargain prices. For a budget-friendly lunch, grab a "bocadillo" (Spanish sandwich) or a delicious "papas arrugadas" (wrinkled potatoes) with "mojo" (Canarian sauce) from one of the food stalls.

Night: Embark on a self-guided "Ruta de Tapas" (Tapas Route) to experience the vibrant nightlife scene of Las Palmas without blowing your budget.

- **Cost:** €10-€20 per person (depending on how many tapas and drinks you order)

Imagine yourself hopping from bar to bar, sampling an array of mouthwatering tapas – small, savory dishes showcasing the best of Canarian cuisine. Start with a glass of the local "vino de la tierra" (wine) and order a few tapas to share. Popular choices include "papas arrugadas con mojo," "pimientos de padrón" (blistered peppers), and "gambas al ajillo" (garlic shrimp). The atmosphere in most tapas bars is lively and friendly, perfect for soaking up the local culture and enjoying a fun night out. Ask the locals for their recommendations on hidden gem tapas bars, which often offer the best deals and tastiest bites.

Day 2: Hiking the Pico de Bandama Caldera and a Relaxing Beach Day

Morning: Lace up your hiking boots and embark on a free hike to the Pico de Bandama Caldera, a volcanic crater offering stunning panoramic views.

- **Address:** Carretera Tamaraceite-Tafira (starting point for the hike)
- **Cost:** Free
- **Directions:** From Las Palmas, take a bus or taxi to Tamaraceite, a small village located northwest of the city. The trailhead for the Pico de Bandama Caldera is easily accessible from the village center.

Imagine yourself following a well-maintained trail through a volcanic landscape dotted with native flora. As you ascend the crater rim, the panoramic views become more breathtaking. Marvel at the vast expanse of the caldera, a reminder of Gran Canaria's volcanic origins. On a clear day, you can see all the way to the neighboring island of Tenerife. The hike itself is moderate and takes approximately 2-3 hours to complete. Don't forget to bring plenty of water and wear comfortable shoes with good grip.

Afternoon: After your invigorating hike, reward yourself with a relaxing afternoon at Las Canteras Beach, a popular urban beach in Las Palmas.

- **Address:** Las Canteras Beach, Las Palmas de Gran Canaria, Spain
- **Cost:** Free to access

Imagine yourself sinking your toes into the golden sand of Las Canteras Beach, feeling the warm Canarian sun on your skin and the cool Atlantic breeze caressing your face. This 3-kilometer stretch of golden sand is a haven for relaxation and offers a variety of activities for budget-conscious travelers.

- **Surfing Paradise:** If you're feeling adventurous, Las Canteras boasts some of the best waves in Gran Canaria for beginner and intermediate surfers. Several surf schools offer affordable lessons and board rentals, allowing you to catch your first wave or hone your skills.

- **Snorkeling Adventure:** For a more low-key activity, explore the underwater world teeming with colorful fish and marine life. The volcanic rock formations at the northern end of the beach create a natural reef system, perfect for snorkeling. You can rent basic snorkeling equipment from vendors on the beach for a reasonable price.
- **Sunbathing Bliss:** If relaxation is your priority, simply grab a beach towel or rent a sunbed and umbrella (around €5 each) and soak up the sun. Read a captivating book, listen to your favorite music, or simply close your eyes and let the soothing sounds of the waves lull you into a state of tranquility.

Beyond the Beach:

Las Canteras Beach offers more than just sand and surf. Take a stroll along the scenic beachfront promenade lined with palm trees and cafes. Stop for a refreshing drink or a delicious ice cream while people-watching and enjoying the vibrant atmosphere. For a touch of history, visit the La Cicer observation deck located at the northern end of the beach. This former military fortification offers panoramic views of the coastline and the city. Entry is free, making it a perfect budget-friendly activity.

Night:

As the sun sets, painting the sky in vibrant hues of orange and pink, head to one of Las Canteras Beach's many beachfront restaurants for a delicious and affordable dinner. Many restaurants offer "menús del día" (set menus) featuring traditional Canarian cuisine at a fixed price. Enjoy fresh seafood dishes, local cheeses, and regional specialties while savoring the breathtaking ocean views.

(Optional Activity): For a touch of excitement, join a lively "fiesta" (festival) happening in Las Palmas. Gran Canaria boasts a vibrant cultural scene with frequent street festivals, concerts, and open-air performances. These events are typically free or very affordable and offer a fantastic opportunity to immerse yourself in the local culture and experience the island's infectious energy.

Day 3: Exploring Arucas and a Local Food Extravaganza

Morning: Take a day trip to the charming town of Arucas, renowned for its historical significance and its production of "ron miel" (honey rum).

- **Address:** Arucas, Arucas Municipality, Spain
- **Cost:** Free to explore the town, entry fees for museums may apply
- **Directions:** From Las Palmas, take a bus or rent a car to Arucas. The journey takes approximately 30 minutes and offers scenic views of the countryside.

Imagine yourself strolling through the cobbled streets of Arucas, admiring the colorful houses with intricate balconies and decorative facades. Visit the iconic Iglesia de San Juan Bautista, a magnificent neoclassical church that dominates the town square. For a deeper dive into the town's history, consider visiting the Museo Municipal de Arucas, housed in a beautifully restored 17th-century mansion. Entry fees are typically minimal and offer fascinating insights into Arucas' rich heritage.

Afternoon: No exploration of Arucas is complete without experiencing its most famous product – "ron miel." Head to the renowned "Arehucas Factory," a family-run distillery that has been producing this popular rum for over 130 years. Many companies offer guided tours of the distillery, showcasing the rum-making process from sugarcane harvesting to the final bottling. The tours typically end with a tasting session, allowing you to sample different varieties of "ron miel" and discover your favorite. While there are usually small fees associated with the tours, they offer a unique experience and a chance to learn about a significant aspect of Canarian culture.

Night: For your final night in Gran Canaria, treat yourself to a delicious and affordable feast at a "Guachinche" (traditional Canarian restaurant).

- **Cost:** €15-€20 per person (depending on the menu and drinks)

Imagine yourself nestled in a cozy, family-run restaurant, surrounded by locals enjoying a lively atmosphere. Guachinches often serve their dishes "family style," with large platters placed in the center of the table for everyone to share. This is a fantastic way to try a variety of Canarian specialties and experience the local way of dining. Don't be afraid to ask the friendly staff for recommendations and recommendations on pairing the dishes with local wines. Many Guachinches offer their own "vino de la tierra" or a selection of regional wines at very reasonable prices.

Beyond the Feast:

The atmosphere in Guachinches is often lively and welcoming. Locals come together to enjoy good food, conversation, and traditional music. You might even get a chance to try your hand at a local dance or simply soak up the infectious energy of the place. Guachinches are typically open on weekends and evenings, so plan your visit accordingly.

Post-Dinner Stargazing Adventure:

After your delicious feast, escape the city lights and head to a designated "Starlight Tourist Zone" for a truly magical experience: stargazing in Gran Canaria.

- **Cost:** Free (although some stargazing tours may have a fee)

Imagine yourself lying on a blanket under a blanket of stars, feeling a sense of awe and wonder at the vastness of the universe. Due to its minimal light pollution and clear skies, Gran Canaria is one of the best places in Europe for stargazing. Head to a designated "Starlight Tourist Zone" like Tamadaba National Park or Degollada de la Cumbre. Here, you can marvel at the Milky Way in all its glory, spot planets twinkling in the distance, and witness constellations you never knew existed. Several companies offer guided stargazing tours with telescopes and expert commentary, adding to the immersive experience. While some tours come with a fee, there are also free stargazing events organized by local astronomy clubs. Do some research beforehand to find a free event happening during your visit.

The End of a Budget-Friendly Adventure:

As your 3-day adventure in Gran Canaria draws to a close, you'll be filled with unforgettable memories and a newfound appreciation for this beautiful island. You've explored charming towns, discovered hidden beaches, immersed yourself in the local culture, and all without breaking the bank. Gran Canaria truly offers something for everyone, and with a little planning and resourcefulness, you can experience its magic on a budget. So, pack your bags, embrace your adventurous spirit, and get ready to create your own budget-friendly Gran Canaria adventure!

Historical and Cultural Immersion Itinerary

Gran Canaria isn't just about stunning beaches and volcanic landscapes; it's a treasure trove of history and vibrant culture. Imagine yourself wandering through cobbled streets lined with colonial architecture, delving into fascinating museums, and experiencing age-old traditions that continue to shape the island's identity. This 3-day itinerary caters to the history buff and culture enthusiast, offering a journey through time that will leave you with a deeper appreciation for Gran Canaria's unique heritage.

Day 1: Unveiling the Legacy of Vegueta and a Celebration of Canarian Folklore

Morning: Start your historical adventure with a free walking tour through Vegueta, the enchanting historic center of Las Palmas de Gran Canaria.

- **Address:** Plaza de Santa Ana, Las Palmas de Gran Canaria, Spain (starting point for most free walking tours)
- **Cost:** Free (optional tips for the guide at the end)

- **Directions:** Most resorts in Gran Canaria offer bus connections to Las Palmas. Alternatively, take a taxi or rent a car. Free walking tours typically start from Plaza de Santa Ana, located in the heart of Vegueta.

Imagine yourself strolling through narrow cobbled streets lined with colorful colonial buildings. Your knowledgeable guide will unveil the rich history of Vegueta, pointing out landmarks like the magnificent Santa Ana Cathedral, the Casa de Colón (Columbus House), and the Palacio Episcopal (Bishop's Palace). Learn about the island's indigenous culture, the arrival of Christopher Columbus, and the architectural influences that have shaped the city. These free walking tours are a fantastic way to orient yourself in the city, discover hidden gems, and gain local insights without spending a dime.

Afternoon: After your walking tour, delve deeper into Gran Canaria's pre-Hispanic past at the CAAM (Museo Canario).

- **Address:** Calle Doctor Juan Bosch Millares, 35, Las Palmas de Gran Canaria, Spain
- **Cost:** €4 (general admission)
- **Directions:** The CAAM is located within walking distance of most landmarks in Vegueta.

Imagine yourself engrossed in intricate pottery designs, each piece whispering stories of daily life and rituals. Marvel at delicate jewelry crafted from shells and volcanic stones, a testament to the Guanches' artistic skills. Stand face-to-face with well-preserved mummies, their expressions offering a glimpse into the past. Interactive exhibits bring the island's pre-Hispanic history to life, allowing you to participate in grinding corn using traditional tools or decipher the meaning behind ancient symbols. Informative displays, often accompanied by audio guides in multiple languages, provide in-depth explanations about the Guanche culture, their social structure, and their unique relationship with the island's environment.

Beyond the Exhibits:

The CAAM offers more than just a static collection of artifacts. Consider attending a temporary exhibition showcasing contemporary Canarian art or participate in a guided tour led by a knowledgeable museum staff member. These tours, offered at an additional cost, delve deeper into specific aspects of Guanche culture or explore the museum's permanent collection in greater detail. The museum also boasts a charming rooftop cafe with stunning panoramic views of Vegueta. Enjoy a refreshing drink or a light lunch while soaking in the historical ambiance and the vibrant city below.

Night:

Immerse yourself in the vibrant tapestry of Canarian folklore with a lively "Noche de Fiesta" (festive night) in Vegueta.

- **Cost:** Varies depending on the venue and activities; some events are free, while others may have entrance fees.

Imagine yourself strolling through the bustling streets of Vegueta, the air filled with the infectious rhythm of traditional music. Street performers dressed in colorful attire showcase their talents, playing instruments like the "timple" (a small Canarian guitar) and the "chácaras" (hand-clappers). Local dance groups perform energetic folkloric dances, their elaborate costumes and synchronized movements captivating the audience. Many restaurants and bars host special "Noche de Fiesta" evenings, offering traditional Canarian cuisine alongside live music and dance performances. Join the crowd, sample local delicacies, and lose yourself in the infectious rhythm of Canarian culture. Be sure to inquire with your hotel or local tourist office about upcoming "Noche de Fiesta" events happening during your stay.

Day 2: A Journey Through Colonial Grandeur and a Culinary Adventure

Morning: Travel back in time to the opulent era of the Spanish conquest with a visit to the Casa de Colón (Columbus House).

- **Address:** Calle Colón, 1, Las Palmas de Gran Canaria, Spain
- **Cost:** €3 (general admission)
- **Directions:** The Casa de Colón is located within walking distance of most landmarks in Vegueta.

Imagine yourself stepping into the grand 15th-century mansion that once served as Christopher Columbus's residence on his voyages to the New World. The meticulously restored house showcases period furniture, maps, and nautical instruments, offering a glimpse into the life and times of this famous explorer. Interactive exhibits and informative displays shed light on Columbus's connection to Gran Canaria and the crucial role the island played in his voyages. As you wander through the rooms, imagine the conversations that took place within these walls and the historical significance of this architectural gem.

Afternoon: After your historical exploration, embark on a culinary adventure at Mercado Central de Las Palmas, a bustling market overflowing with fresh local produce and delectable Canarian specialties.

- **Address:** Calle Luis Morote, Las Palmas de Gran Canaria, Spain
- **Cost:** Free to enter, prices for food and drinks vary

Imagine yourself navigating through a maze of colorful stalls, the air filled with the enticing aroma of spices and freshly baked bread. Sample exotic fruits you've never seen before, like the sweet and tangy "mango" or the refreshing "papaya." Admire the vibrant displays of locally grown vegetables, from the plump "tomates cherry" (cherry tomatoes) to the unique "papas negras" (black potatoes) grown in volcanic soil. For lunch, indulge in a delicious "gofio escaldado" (a porridge made from roasted gofio flour), a local staple dish, or grab a selection of tapas to share, showcasing the diverse flavors of Canarian cuisine. Don't forget to try a glass of the local "vino de la tierra" (wine) for a truly authentic culinary experience.

Night: Enjoy a gourmet dinner with a historical twist at a restaurant specializing in traditional Canarian cuisine.

- **Cost:** €20-€40 per person (depending on the restaurant and menu choices)

Imagine yourself nestled in a charming restaurant tucked away in a cobbled street of Vegueta. The warm glow of candlelight illuminates the room, adorned with traditional Canarian artwork and woven tapestries. Live music, featuring the melancholic melodies of the "timple" and the rhythmic clinking of "chácaras," creates a captivating ambiance. Peruse the menu, filled with dishes that have been passed down through generations, each a testament to the island's rich culinary heritage.

A Feast for the Senses:

Start your gastronomic adventure with a selection of tempting appetizers. Sample "papas arrugadas con mojo," a quintessential Canarian dish featuring small wrinkled potatoes served with flavorful red and green "mojo" sauces. Indulge in "queso asado" (grilled cheese) made from local sheep or goat's milk, its smoky aroma whetting your appetite. For a seafood option, try "almejas a la marinera" (clams in a garlicky white wine sauce), the fresh ocean flavors bursting in your mouth.

The Main Course Delights:

For your main course, delve deeper into the heart of Canarian cuisine. Meat lovers can savor "carne fiesta," a slow-cooked stew traditionally made with pork, chorizo sausage, and chickpeas. For a lighter option, try "pescado a la plancha" (grilled fish), the fresh catch of the day cooked to perfection and seasoned with simple herbs and olive oil. Vegetarians can enjoy "ropa vieja" (a chickpea and vegetable stew) or "escaldón" (a gofio porridge dish with vegetables and cheese).

A Sweet Ending:

No Canarian meal is complete without a traditional dessert. Treat yourself to "bienmesabe," a sweet almond pudding flavored with cinnamon and rum, or "truchas de batata" (sweet potato fritters) drizzled with honey. Pair your dessert with a glass of the local "vino dulce" (sweet wine) for a truly decadent finale.

Beyond the Food:

Many restaurants specializing in traditional cuisine offer a glimpse into Canarian culture beyond the plate. Inquire about live music performances featuring local musicians or folkloric dance shows that might be happening during your visit. These evenings provide a delightful opportunity to immerse yourself in the island's vibrant cultural tapestry while enjoying a delicious and authentic meal.

Art and Architecture Delights

Gran Canaria isn't just about sun-drenched beaches and dramatic landscapes; it's a haven for art enthusiasts and architecture aficionados. Imagine yourself wandering through galleries bursting with contemporary creations, delving into museums that unveil the island's artistic heritage, and marveling at architectural wonders that whisper stories of different eras. This 3-day itinerary caters to the creative soul, offering a journey through artistic expression and architectural marvels that will leave you inspired and invigorated.

Day 1: Unveiling the Artistic Tapestry of Vegueta and a Sunset Serenade

Morning: Start your artistic adventure with a free walking tour through Vegueta, the enchanting historic heart of Las Palmas de Gran Canaria.

- **Address:** Plaza de Santa Ana, Las Palmas de Gran Canaria, Spain (starting point for most free walking tours)
- **Cost:** Free (optional tips for the guide at the end)
- **Directions:** Most resorts in Gran Canaria offer bus connections to Las Palmas. Alternatively, take a taxi or rent a car. Free walking tours typically start from Plaza de Santa Ana, located in the heart of Vegueta.

Imagine yourself strolling through narrow cobbled streets lined with colorful colonial buildings, each one an architectural gem. Your knowledgeable guide will point out landmarks like the magnificent Santa Ana Cathedral, a masterpiece of Canarian architecture with its intricate facade and stained-glass windows. Learn about the historical influences that shaped the city's architectural style, from the traditional Canarian houses with their wooden balconies to the imposing neoclassical buildings that stand as testaments to the island's colonial past.

Afternoon: After your walking tour, delve deeper into Gran Canaria's artistic soul at the Centro Atlántico de Arte Moderno (CAAM).

- **Address:** Calle Doctor Juan Bosch Millares, 35, Las Palmas de Gran Canaria, Spain
- **Cost:** €4 (general admission)
- **Directions:** The CAAM is located within walking distance of most landmarks in Vegueta.

Imagine yourself surrounded by captivating works of modern and contemporary art from Spain and the Canary Islands. The museum houses a permanent collection showcasing paintings, sculptures, and installations by renowned artists like Martín Chirino and Manolo Millares. Temporary exhibitions offer a platform for emerging talent and explore diverse artistic movements. Interactive displays and informative audio guides (available in multiple languages) allow you to delve deeper into the meaning behind the art and gain insights into the artistic landscape of the Canary Islands.

Night: Immerse yourself in a unique artistic experience with a "Noche de Ópera" (Opera Night) at the Teatro Pérez Galdós, a magnificent neoclassical theater.

- **Address:** Calle Domingo Jentkins, s/n, Las Palmas de Gran Canaria, Spain
- **Cost:** Ticket prices vary depending on the performance (check the theater's website for current listings)

- **Directions:** The Teatro Pérez Galdós is located within walking distance of most landmarks in Vegueta.

Imagine yourself dressed to impress, entering the grand theater with its ornate ceilings and plush red seats. The anticipation builds as the lights dim and the orchestra begins to play. Lose yourself in the beauty of a captivating opera performance, be it a timeless classic by Verdi or Puccini or a contemporary piece by a Spanish composer. The passionate voices of the singers, the powerful music, and the stunning stage production create a truly magical and unforgettable experience. Check the theater's website for upcoming performances during your stay and book your tickets in advance, especially during peak season.

Day 2: A Journey Through Modern Masterpieces and a Hidden Architectural Gem

Morning: Escape the bustling city and head to the serene Cactualdea Park, a unique botanical garden dedicated to cacti and succulents.

- **Address:** Barranco de Guiniguada, Km 7, Arucas, Spain
- **Cost:** €6 (general admission)
- **Directions:** From Las Palmas, take a bus or rent a car to Arucas. Cactualdea Park is located a short taxi ride from the town center.

Imagine yourself strolling through a meticulously landscaped garden, a wonderland of cacti and succulents in all shapes and sizes. Towering cacti reaching for the sky, vibrant aloe vera plants, and whimsical euphorbias create a surreal and captivating landscape. Learn about the diverse flora adapted to Gran Canaria's arid climate and discover the unique beauty of these resilient plants. Cactualdea Park is not just a botanical garden; it's also a work of art. Sculptures seamlessly integrated into the landscape add another layer of artistic expression and create a harmonious blend of nature and human creativity.

Afternoon: In the afternoon, head to Puerto de Mogán, a charming harbor town in the southwest of Gran Canaria, and explore the Mogán Art & Culture Center.

- **Address:** Calle Ernesto Sarti Martín 1, Local 2, Puerto de Mogán, Mogán Municipality, Spain
- **Cost:** Free entry for the exhibition space, prices for workshops and events may vary
- **Directions:** From Arucas, take a taxi or rent a car to Puerto de Mogán. The Mogán Art & Culture Center is located in the heart of the town's marina area.

Imagine yourself walking through a beautifully restored traditional Canarian house, transformed into a vibrant art space. The Mogán Art & Culture Center showcases a diverse range of contemporary art by local and international artists. Paintings, sculptures, and installations explore a variety of themes, from the island's natural beauty to social commentary. The center also hosts workshops and events throughout the year, offering opportunities to learn about art, participate in creative activities, and interact with local artists.

Night: Enjoy a delightful dinner with a view at a restaurant overlooking Puerto de Mogán's picturesque harbor.

- **Cost:** €20-€40 per person (depending on the restaurant and menu choices)

Imagine yourself nestled on a restaurant terrace, the gentle sea breeze caressing your face as you savor a delicious meal. Colorful fishing boats bob gently in the water, and the twinkling lights of the town illuminate the harbor. As you dine, be sure to inquire about any live music performances happening that night. Local musicians often play traditional Canarian music or contemporary tunes, adding to the enchanting atmosphere of the evening. After dinner, take a leisurely stroll along the harbor front, soaking in the beauty of the surroundings and the peaceful ambiance.

Day 3: A Glimpse into Aboriginal Architecture and a Farewell Fiesta

Morning: Travel back in time to discover the fascinating Cenobio de Valerón, a network of ancient caves used by the island's indigenous inhabitants, the Guanches.

- **Address:** Km 7.5 Autopista del Sur, Santa María de Guía de Gran Canaria, Spain
- **Cost:** €5 (general admission)
- **Directions:** From Puerto de Mogán, take a taxi or rent a car and drive south on the GC-1 motorway. The Cenobio de Valerón is well signposted and easily accessible.

Imagine yourself descending into a series of naturally formed caves, remnants of a unique architectural achievement by the Guanches. These caves were used for various purposes, including grain storage, religious ceremonies, and even burials. Informative displays and guided tours (available at an additional cost) shed light on the lives of the Guanches, their ingenuity in utilizing natural resources, and the significance of these caves in their culture. As you explore the network of caves, imagine the whispers of history echoing through the chambers and feel a sense of connection to the island's ancient past.

Afternoon: After your historical exploration, head back to Las Palmas and indulge in a final cultural experience at Casa-Museo Pérez Galdós, a museum dedicated to the life and works of renowned Spanish novelist Benito Pérez Galdós.

- **Address:** Calle Cano 2, Las Palmas de Gran Canaria, Spain
- **Cost:** €3 (general admission)
- **Directions:** The Casa-Museo Pérez Galdós is located within walking distance of most landmarks in Vegueta.

Imagine yourself stepping into the elegantly restored 19th-century home of Benito Pérez Galdós, a literary giant of Spain. The museum houses a collection of his personal belongings, manuscripts, and first editions, offering a glimpse into his life and creative process.

The Casa-Museo Pérez Galdós offers a captivating window into the life and works of Benito Pérez Galdós, a literary giant of Spain. Imagine yourself stepping into the elegantly restored 19th-century home, its rooms adorned with period furniture, paintings, and personal items that belonged to Galdós. Exhibits showcase his manuscripts, first editions, and even handwritten correspondence, allowing you to connect with the author on a deeper level. Informative displays (often accompanied by audio guides in multiple languages) delve into Galdós' literary career, his influences, and the social and political commentary woven into his novels.

Beyond the Exhibits:

The Casa-Museo Pérez Galdós offers more than just a static collection of artifacts. Consider attending a temporary exhibition exploring a specific theme in Galdós' work or participate in a guided tour led by a knowledgeable museum staff member. These tours, offered at an additional cost, delve deeper into his life, his writing process, and the historical context that shaped his novels. The museum also boasts a charming library with a curated selection of Galdós' works and books related to his life and times. Spend some time here, browsing the shelves or immersing yourself in a chapter of one of his novels.

Night: Bid farewell to Gran Canaria with a lively "Fiesta de Despedida" (Farewell Party) in Vegueta.

- **Cost:** Varies depending on the venue and activities; some events are free, while others may have entrance fees.

Imagine yourself joining the vibrant throng in Vegueta's bustling streets, the air filled with music, laughter, and the infectious energy of a celebration. Street performers dressed in colorful traditional costumes showcase their talents, while local musicians play lively tunes that make you want to move. Restaurants and bars offer special "Fiesta de Despedida" menus with traditional Canarian cuisine and refreshing local drinks. Join a group of locals, learn a few basic dance steps, and lose yourself in the joyous atmosphere. As the night unfolds, savor the delicious food, soak in the vibrant culture, and create lasting memories of your time in Gran Canaria. Be sure to inquire with your hotel or local tourist office about upcoming "Fiesta de Despedida" events happening during your last night.

Family Fun Itinerary

Gran Canaria isn't just a haven for sun-worshippers and romance-seekers; it's a playground waiting to be explored by families with children of all ages. Imagine the excitement on your children's faces as they build sandcastles on pristine beaches, encounter fascinating creatures at marine parks, and embark on exciting adventures through volcanic landscapes. This 3-day itinerary caters to the entire family, offering a perfect blend of relaxation, learning, and thrilling activities that will create lasting memories for everyone.

Day 1: A Splashing Good Time at Aqualand Maspalomas and a Family Fiesta

Morning: Make a splash at Aqualand Maspalomas, the largest water park in Gran Canaria.

- **Address:** Autopista del Sur Km 53, Maspalomas, San Bartolomé de Tirajana, Spain
- **Cost:** €29 (adults), €23 (children aged 9-11), free for children under 9 (prices may vary depending on the season; check the Aqualand Maspalomas website for current rates)
- **Directions:** Most resorts in Gran Canaria offer bus connections to Maspalomas. Alternatively, take a taxi or rent a car. The water park is well signposted and easily accessible.

Imagine yourself and your children squealing with delight as you plummet down thrilling water slides, race each other on lazy rivers, and float

peacefully in wave pools. Aqualand Maspalomas offers a variety of attractions for all ages, from heart-stopping slides like the "Boomerang" and the "Twister" to kid-friendly splash pools and a dedicated children's area. Don't forget the sun cream, swimsuits, and towels! Lockers and changing rooms are available for rent within the park.

Afternoon: After drying off at the water park, head to Playa del Inglés, a beautiful sandy beach located next to Maspalomas.

- **Address:** Playa del Inglés, San Bartolomé de Tirajana, Spain (access to the beach is free)
- **Directions:** Playa del Inglés is a short walk or taxi ride from Aqualand Maspalomas.

Imagine yourself relaxing on the golden sand with your family, the gentle waves lapping at your feet. Build sandcastles together, play beach volleyball, or simply soak up the sun and enjoy the refreshing sea breeze. For the more adventurous family members, try out water sports like kayaking, windsurfing, or stand-up paddleboarding (lessons and rentals are available).

Night: Immerse yourselves in a vibrant "Fiesta Canaria" (Canarian Festival) in Playa del Inglés.

- **Cost:** Free to walk around and enjoy the atmosphere; prices for food and drinks vary

Imagine yourself strolling through a lively street market filled with colorful stalls selling traditional Canarian crafts and souvenirs. The air is filled with the infectious rhythm of traditional music as local dance groups perform energetic folkloric dances in elaborate costumes. Children will be mesmerized by the vibrant atmosphere and playful street performers. Many restaurants and bars offer special "Fiesta Canaria" menus, allowing you to sample delicious local cuisine while enjoying live music and family-friendly entertainment. Look out for posters or ask your hotel reception for information about upcoming "Fiesta Canaria" events happening during your stay.

Day 2: Camel Rides Through the Dunes and a Night Under the Stars

Morning: Embark on a unique adventure through the Maspalomas Dunes, a vast expanse of golden sand reminiscent of the Sahara Desert.

- **Address:** Campo Internacional Maspalomas, Maspalomas, San Bartolomé de Tirajana, Spain (most camel ride companies are located near the Campo Internacional roundabout)
- **Cost:** €20-€25 per person (prices may vary depending on the duration of the ride)
- **Directions:** Most resorts in Gran Canaria offer bus connections to Maspalomas. Alternatively, take a taxi or rent a car. The Maspalomas Dunes are located near the Campo Internacional roundabout. Several camel ride companies operate in the area, and their staff will be easily identifiable with stalls or flags.

Imagine yourself perched atop a gentle giant, a camel, as you traverse the rolling sand dunes of Maspalomas. This unique and exhilarating experience allows you to explore the desert-like landscape from a different perspective. Many companies offer short rides perfect for families with young children, while longer adventures cater to those seeking a more in-depth exploration. As you ride, keep an eye out for interesting plant life adapted to the dry conditions and marvel at the breathtaking views of the coastline.

Afternoon: After your camel ride, head to Palmitos Park, a botanical and zoological garden offering a fun and educational experience for the whole family.

- **Address:** Barranco de los Palmitos, s/n, Maspalomas, San Bartolomé de Tirajana, Spain
- **Cost:** €24 (adults), €18 (children aged 3-10), free for children under 3 (prices may vary depending on the season; check the Palmitos Park website for current rates)
- **Directions:** Palmitos Park is located a short taxi ride from the Maspalomas Dunes.

Imagine yourself surrounded by lush vegetation from around the world, exploring themed gardens filled with exotic flowers, cascading waterfalls, and vibrant birdlife. Palmitos Park offers a variety of attractions, including a dolphin show, a raptor exhibition showcasing birds of prey, and even a butterfly house teeming with colorful winged creatures. Children will be delighted by the opportunity to see a variety of animals up close, from playful monkeys to majestic parrots. The park also boasts a petting zoo where children can interact with gentle creatures like goats, sheep, and rabbits.

Night: Enjoy a stargazing adventure at a designated stargazing location with a guided tour.

- **Cost:** €15-€25 per person (prices may vary depending on the company and the tour inclusions)
- **Directions:** Several companies offer guided stargazing tours in Gran Canaria. They typically pick you up from your hotel or a central location and transport you to a dark location with minimal light pollution, often in the mountains.

Imagine yourself lying on a blanket under a sky ablaze with a million twinkling stars. A knowledgeable guide will point out constellations, planets, and other celestial objects, sharing fascinating facts about the universe. This unique experience allows families to reconnect with nature and appreciate the awe-inspiring beauty of the night sky. Many tours offer telescopes for a closer look at the stars and planets, and some may even include snacks or hot drinks to enhance the experience. Be sure to book your stargazing tour in advance, especially during peak season.

Day 3: A Pirate Adventure and a Relaxing Beach Day

Morning: Set sail on a thrilling pirate adventure cruise departing from Puerto Rico.

- **Address:** Puerto Rico de Gran Canaria, Mogán Municipality, Spain (most cruise companies operate from the main harbor area)

- **Cost:** €30-€40 per person (prices may vary depending on the company and the duration of the cruise)
- **Directions:** Most resorts in Gran Canaria offer bus connections to Puerto Rico. Alternatively, take a taxi or rent a car. The Puerto Rico harbor is well signposted and easily accessible.

Imagine yourself and your children transformed into swashbuckling pirates embarking on a high-seas adventure. These themed cruises offer a fun-filled experience with pirate games, face painting, and exciting stories about buried treasure. As you sail along the coast, keep an eye out for dolphins and other marine life. Many cruises include a refreshing swim stop in a secluded cove, allowing families to cool off and enjoy a bit of snorkeling.

Afternoon: After your pirate adventure, spend a relaxing afternoon at Playa de Amadores, a sheltered beach known for its calm waters and pristine golden sand.

- **Address:** Playa de Amadores, Mogán Municipality, Spain (access to the beach is free)

Directions: Playa de Amadores is a short taxi ride or bus journey from Puerto Rico. The beach is well signposted and easily accessible by car as well.

Imagine yourself relaxing on a sun lounger with your family, the gentle waves lapping at the shore. Playa de Amadores boasts calm, shallow waters, making it perfect for families with young children. Build sandcastles together, splash in the refreshing water, or simply soak up the sun and enjoy the beautiful scenery. For the more adventurous, try out water sports like kayaking, paddleboarding, or banana boat rides (rentals are available on the beach). Several restaurants and cafes line the beachfront, offering delicious snacks, refreshing drinks, and ice cream - perfect for a post-beach treat.

Night: Enjoy a farewell dinner with a local flair at a traditional Canarian restaurant.

- **Cost:** €20-€40 per person (depending on the restaurant and menu choices)

Imagine yourself tucked away in a charming restaurant with rustic décor, the scent of freshly baked bread and grilled fish filling the air. End your Gran Canaria adventure with a delicious meal showcasing the island's culinary delights. Sample "papas arrugadas" (wrinkled potatoes) with "mojo" (spicy sauce), "gofio escaldado" (a porridge made from roasted gofio flour), or fresh fish caught locally. Many restaurants offer vegetarian and kid-friendly options to cater to all palates. Live music with traditional instruments like the "timple" (a small Canarian guitar) may add a touch of ambiance to your evening. As you savor the food and the atmosphere, reminisce about the adventures you shared as a family and create lasting memories that you will cherish for years to come.

Festivals and Events: Celebrating Gran Canaria's Spirit

Gran Canaria's vibrant culture comes alive throughout the year with a dazzling array of festivals and events. From lively carnivals and religious processions to traditional music showcases and gastronomic celebrations, there's something for everyone to experience the island's infectious energy.

Here's a glimpse into some of the most popular festivals and events that will immerse you in the heart of Gran Canaria's spirit:

1. Carnival: (February)

Festival: Carnival **Location:** Las Palmas de Gran Canaria (the capital city) and tourist resorts across the island **Date:** February (exact dates vary each year) **Activities:** Elaborate parades with colorful costumes, energetic dance troupes, lively music performances, drag queen competitions, and street parties.

Tips for Visitors: Don't miss the dazzling "cabalgata anunciadora" (announcing parade) marking the official start of Carnival. Come dressed up in a costume and join the vibrant street parties. Be prepared for large crowds and book your accommodation well in advance, especially in Las Palmas.

2. Fiesta del Pino: (September)

Festival: Fiesta del Pino (Festival of the Pine) **Location:** Teror, a town in the central mountains of Gran Canaria **Date:** Third Sunday of September **Activities:** A week-long celebration honoring the Virgin del Pino, the island's patron saint. Features a grand religious procession, traditional music and dance performances, a vibrant market selling local crafts and food, and a spectacular fireworks display.

Tips for Visitors: Witness the "romería" (pilgrimage) on the Sunday of the festival, where thousands of devotees walk from various parts of the island to Teror. Sample the local "bienmesabe" (almond and honey dessert) and explore the charming town of Teror.

3. WOMAD Gran Canaria: (November)

Festival: WOMAD Gran Canaria (World of Music, Arts and Dance) **Location:** Las Palmas de Gran Canaria **Date:** Typically held in November (exact dates vary each year) **Activities:** A global celebration of music, featuring renowned artists from around the world performing diverse genres like reggae, folk, jazz, and world music. Alongside the music, there are dance performances, workshops, art installations, and a vibrant food market offering international cuisine.

Tips for Visitors: Purchase tickets in advance, especially for headline acts. Bring comfortable shoes as you'll be standing and moving around a lot. The festival offers a diverse range of food and drinks, so come hungry and thirsty!

4. Festival Internacional Canarias Jazz & Más: (July)

Jazz & Más (Canary Islands International Jazz & More Festival) **Location:** Various venues across Gran Canaria, with the main concentration in Las Palmas **Date:** Typically held in July (exact dates vary each year) **Activities:** A renowned jazz festival showcasing international and local jazz musicians. The festival also features other musical genres like blues, soul, and funk, creating a diverse and exciting program. Concerts take place in various venues, from open-air stages to intimate jazz bars.

Tips for Visitors: Check the festival program to discover performances that suit your musical taste. Tickets for some of the headline acts can sell out quickly, so book in advance. Many venues offer delicious food and drinks, allowing you to enjoy a complete evening of entertainment.

5. Noche de San Juan: (June 23rd)

Festival: Noche de San Juan (Night of Saint John) **Location:** Beaches across Gran Canaria **Date:** June 23rd **Activities:** A magical night celebrating the summer solstice. People gather on beaches at sunset to light bonfires, jump over the flames for good luck, and watch spectacular fireworks displays.

Tips for Visitors: Arrive at the beach early to secure a good spot. Bring a picnic basket and drinks to enjoy the evening. Participate in the tradition of jumping over the bonfires to cleanse yourself and welcome good luck for the coming year. Be mindful of safety around the bonfires and respect the local customs.

6. Festival Internacional de Teatro de Calle: (May)

Festival: Festival Internacional de Teatro de Calle (International Street Theater Festival) **Location:** Various locations in Santa Lucía de Tirajana, a town in the south of Gran Canaria **Date:** Typically held in May (exact dates vary each year) **Activities:** A lively celebration of street theater featuring international and local performance companies. Expect a vibrant mix of acrobatics, mime, dance, music, and comedy performed on open-air stages and interactive installations throughout the town.

Tips for Visitors: Wear comfortable shoes as you'll be walking around town to see different performances. Bring sunscreen and a hat if the weather is hot. Most performances are free or have a minimal entrance fee, making it an affordable and entertaining activity for the whole family.

7. Día de Canarias: (May 30th)

Festival: Día de Canarias (Canary Islands Day) **Location:** Across Gran Canaria, with major celebrations in Las Palmas and other municipalities **Date:** May 30th **Activities:** A public holiday celebrating the unique culture and heritage of the Canary Islands. Features traditional music and dance performances, folk games, exhibitions showcasing local crafts and products, and street markets overflowing with delicious Canarian food and drinks.

Tips for Visitors: Sample the local "gofio escaldado" (a porridge made from roasted gofio flour) and other Canarian delicacies. Participate in traditional games like "lucha canaria" (Canarian wrestling) or "salto del pastor" (shepherd's jump). Immerse yourself in the festive atmosphere and enjoy the vibrant street performances.

8. Noche de los Balcones: (July)

Festival: Noche de los Balcones (Night of the Balconies) **Location:** Agaete, a town in the northwest of Gran Canaria **Date:** Third Saturday of July **Activities:** A unique and colorful festival celebrating the Virgin del Carmen, the patron saint of fishermen. Houses are adorned with carpets made of colorful flower petals and sand, creating stunning visual displays. A vibrant procession winds its way through the town, culminating in a spectacular fireworks display over the harbor.

Tips for Visitors: Arrive early to secure a spot with a good view of the flower carpets and procession. Wear comfortable shoes as you'll likely be standing and walking around a lot. Be prepared for crowds, especially in the town center.

9. Festival Internacional de Cine de Las Palmas de Gran Canaria: (April)

Festival: Festival Internacional de Cine de Las Palmas de Gran Canaria (Las Palmas de Gran Canaria International Film Festival) **Location:** Various cinemas and cultural centers in Las Palmas **Date:** Typically held in April (exact dates vary each year) **Activities:** A prestigious film festival showcasing independent and international films from around the world. Features screenings, premieres, Q&A sessions with filmmakers, workshops, and awards ceremonies.

Tips for Visitors: Purchase tickets in advance for screenings of highly anticipated films. Check the festival program to discover films that suit your taste. This is a great opportunity to experience international cinema and discover new talents.

10. Semana Santa: (Holy Week)

Festival: Semana Santa (Holy Week) **Location:** Across Gran Canaria, with major processions in Las Palmas, Arucas, and Teror **Date:** Varies depending on the lunar calendar (typically falls in March or April) **Activities:** A solemn religious celebration commemorating the Passion and Resurrection of Jesus Christ. Features elaborate processions with costumed participants carrying religious statues, accompanied by somber music and incense.

Tips for Visitors: Respect the religious nature of the event. Dress modestly if you plan to attend processions. Be aware of road closures and detours during processions. This is a good time to experience the island's religious traditions and witness the devotion of the local people.

11. Fiesta de La Rama: (Early August)

Festival: Fiesta de La Rama (Festival of the Branch) **Location:** Agaete, a town in the northwest of Gran Canaria **Date:** First weekend of August **Activities:** A vibrant celebration with a unique historical significance. Reenacts the arrival of a miraculous branch washed ashore in Agaete in the 15th century, believed to be a sign from the Virgin Mary. Features a colorful "rama" (branch) procession adorned with fruits, flowers, and religious symbols, traditional music and dance performances, and a lively street market.

Tips for Visitors: Learn about the historical origin of the festival and its significance to the local people. Sample "bienmesabe," a traditional almond and honey dessert, often sold during the festival. Wear comfortable clothing and shoes as you'll likely be walking and participating in the festivities.

12. Mercado Medieval de Aguimes: (November)

Festival: Mercado Medieval de Aguimes (Aguimes Medieval Market) **Location:** Aguimes, a town in the southeast of Gran Canaria **Date:** Typically held in November (exact dates vary each year) **Activities:** A captivating journey back in time to the medieval era. The town center transforms into a bustling marketplace with stalls selling handcrafted goods, traditional food and drinks, and souvenirs. Costumed performers, musicians, jugglers, and artisans recreate the atmosphere of a medieval marketplace, offering a fun and interactive experience.

Tips for Visitors: Dress up in medieval attire to enhance the experience (optional). Bring cash for purchases at the market stalls. Enjoy live music performances and street entertainment throughout the day.

13. Festival de La Tapa en Tafira: (October)

Festival: Festival de La Tapa en Tafira (The Tapa Festival in Tafira) **Location:** Tafira, a district of Las Palmas de Gran Canaria **Date:** Typically held in October (exact dates vary each year) **Activities:** A celebration of the beloved Spanish tapas, featuring dozens of restaurants and bars offering a wide variety of creative and delicious tapas at affordable prices. Live music creates a vibrant atmosphere as visitors wander from bar to bar, sampling tapas and enjoying the festive ambiance.

Tips for Visitors: Come hungry and thirsty! Purchase a "tapaporte" (tapas passport) which allows you to sample tapas at discounted prices at participating establishments. Be prepared for crowds, especially during peak hours.

14. Brisa Festival: (December)

Festival: Brisa Festival (Breeze Festival) **Location:** Puerto del Mogán, a resort town in the southwest of Gran Canaria **Date:** Typically held in December (exact dates vary each year) **Activities:** A celebration of classical music held in the beautiful setting of Puerto del Mogán. Features international and local classical musicians performing a variety of chamber music concerts and recitals in churches, historical buildings, and open-air venues.

Tips for Visitors: Purchase tickets in advance for concerts, especially for popular artists. Check the festival program to discover performances that suit your musical taste. Dress comfortably but elegantly for the evening concerts.

15. Startup Weekend Gran Canaria: (Varies)

Festival: Startup Weekend Gran Canaria **Location:** Las Palmas de Gran Canaria (specific location varies depending on the event) **Date:** Held multiple times throughout the year **Activities:** A dynamic event fostering entrepreneurship and innovation. Brings together aspiring entrepreneurs, developers, designers, and investors to collaborate on developing new business ideas over a 54-hour weekend. Offers workshops, mentoring sessions, and opportunities to pitch ideas to potential investors.

Tips for Visitors: If you're an entrepreneur or simply interested in innovation, consider participating in the event. Register beforehand to secure your spot. Startup Weekend Gran Canaria is a great platform to network with like-minded individuals and learn about the latest trends in the business world.

Part 6: Beyond the Tourist Trail: Unforgettable Experiences

Hidden Gems & Lesser-Known Destinations:

Gran Canaria offers more than just the popular tourist hotspots. Beyond the bustling beaches and familiar attractions lies a treasure trove of hidden gems waiting to be discovered. From charming villages steeped in tradition to breathtaking natural wonders tucked away from the crowds, this chapter unveils some of Gran Canaria's lesser-known destinations that will leave you feeling like an intrepid explorer.

1. Agaete and the Valley of the Tears:

- **Location:** Agaete, a coastal town in the northwest of Gran Canaria. The Valley of the Tears is located inland from Agaete, accessible by car or taxi.
- **Why Visit:** Agaete is a charming fishing village with a relaxed atmosphere and stunning natural beauty. Explore the harbor lined with colorful fishing boats, wander through the narrow cobbled streets adorned with traditional Canarian houses, and soak up the laid-back vibe. A short distance from the town lies the intriguing Valley of the Tears, a dramatic ravine shrouded in mystery. Legend tells of ancient inhabitants who cried tears that formed the valley's distinctive rock formations. Hike through the scenic landscape, marvel at the volcanic rock cliffs, and enjoy breathtaking panoramic views of the northwest coast.

2. Artenara Caves and the Tamadaba Natural Park:

- **Location:** Artenara, a village nestled in the mountainous heart of Gran Canaria. The Tamadaba Natural Park surrounds Artenara.
- **Why Visit:** Artenara is a haven for nature lovers and history buffs. Explore the fascinating Artenara Caves, a network of ancient dwellings inhabited by

the island's indigenous people, the Guanches. Witness the ingenuity of their architectural techniques and delve into the island's pre-Hispanic past. Artenara is also the gateway to the Tamadaba Natural Park, a vast expanse of pristine laurel forest, a remnant of the ancient Tertiary forests that once covered much of Europe. Hike through the lush green trails, breathe in the fresh mountain air, and encounter unique endemic flora and fauna.

3. Guayadeque Ravine and Cactualdea Park:

- **Location:** Barranco de Guayadeque, a valley located in the central-east of Gran Canaria. Cactualdea Park is situated on the outskirts of Arucas, a town near the valley.
- **Why Visit:** The Guayadeque Ravine is a unique geological wonder with a rich cultural heritage. Explore the network of caves carved into the volcanic cliffs, some of which were used as dwellings by the Guanches and later by the island's inhabitants for storage and even religious purposes. Discover the fascinating history of these cave dwellings and marvel at the ingenuity of their construction. A short distance away lies Cactualdea Park, a botanical paradise dedicated to cacti and succulents. Stroll through meticulously landscaped gardens filled with an astonishing variety of these resilient plants, from towering cacti to vibrant succulents. Learn about the diverse adaptations of these drought-resistant plants and discover the beauty of the arid landscape.

4. Mogán Port and Puerto de las Nieves:

- **Location:** Mogán Port, a picturesque harbor town in the southwest of Gran Canaria. Puerto de las Nieves, a charming fishing village on the northwest coast.
- **Why Visit:** Escape the hustle and bustle of the larger resorts and discover the charm of Mogán Port. Explore the harbor filled with luxurious yachts and traditional fishing boats. Wander through the labyrinthine streets lined with colorful houses and boutiques, and indulge in fresh seafood at one of the many harbourfront restaurants. On the other side of the island, Puerto de las Nieves offers a different kind of charm. This tranquil fishing village

boasts a beautiful black sand beach and a laid-back atmosphere. Enjoy a refreshing swim in the volcanic sand beach, explore the small harbor, and savor a delicious meal at a local restaurant with breathtaking ocean views.

5. Degollada de la Becerra and Pico de las Nieves:

- **Location:** Degollada de la Becerra, a mountain pass in the center of Gran Canaria. Pico de las Nieves, the island's highest peak, is accessible from the pass.
- **Why Visit:** Degollada de la Becerra is a scenic mountain pass offering breathtaking panoramic views of the island's interior. Hike through the dramatic landscape, encounter traditional Canarian villages nestled in the mountains, and enjoy the fresh mountain air. For the more adventurous, a challenging hike leads to the summit of Pico de las Nieves, the highest point on Gran Canaria. On a clear day, be rewarded with stunning panoramic views encompassing the entire island, neighboring islands, and even the distant silhouette of Mount Teide on Tenerife. **Note:** Be sure to check weather conditions before attempting a hike to Pico de las Nieves, as the summit can be subject to strong winds and low visibility.

6. Risco Caído and Los Marteles:

- **Location:** Artenara, Tejeda, and Gáldar municipalities, northwest of Gran Canaria.
- **Why Visit:** Risco Caído and Los Marteles are not just hidden gems; they represent a UNESCO World Heritage Site and a window into Gran Canaria's pre-Hispanic past. This vast archaeological complex encompasses a series of caves, granaries, and other structures built by the island's original inhabitants, the Guanches, between the 2nd century BC and the 15th century AD.

Unveiling the Secrets of the Guanches:

Imagine yourself stepping back in time as you explore the intricate network of caves carved into the volcanic cliffs. These caves served various purposes for the Guanches, from dwellings and storage facilities to sacred sites used for religious ceremonies and rituals. Marvel at the ingenuity of their construction techniques, utilizing natural materials and adapting to the challenging terrain. Discover the "casas pintadas" (painted houses), caves adorned with geometric symbols and depictions of animals, offering a glimpse into the Guanches' belief systems and artistic expression.

Los Graneros (The Granaries):

Scattered across the landscape of Risco Caído are numerous "graneros" (granaries), impressive collective storage chambers used by the Guanches to safeguard their crops. These unique structures, some perched precariously on cliffs, were designed to be difficult to access, protecting precious resources like barley and figs. Admire the skilled craftsmanship of these dry-stone constructions, testament to the Guanches' ability to utilize their environment for survival.

The Roque Bentayga:

Rising majestically above the archaeological complex is the Roque Bentayga, a volcanic rock formation with a significant place in Guanche culture. The Roque Bentayga is believed to have served as a sacred sanctuary and astronomical observatory. Observe the numerous petroglyphs (rock carvings) adorning the Roque, depicting geometric patterns, spirals, and pod-like shapes. The exact meaning of these carvings remains a mystery, but they are believed to have held religious or astronomical significance for the Guanches.

Exploring the Cultural Landscape:

Tips for Visitors:

- Several visitor centers offer informative exhibits and guided tours to enhance your understanding of the Risco Caído and Los Marteles complex.
- Moderate hiking trails weave through the landscape, allowing you to explore the archaeological sites at your own pace.
- Wear sturdy shoes suitable for uneven terrain and sun protection as the area receives minimal shade.
- Respect the archaeological significance of the site and avoid disturbing any artifacts or structures.

A Visit to Risco Caído and Los Marteles is not just a journey through a historical site; it's a captivating exploration of a bygone era. Through the well-preserved structures and enigmatic symbols, you gain a deeper appreciation for the ingenuity and cultural richness of the island's indigenous people. This UNESCO World Heritage Site is a hidden gem waiting to be discovered by those seeking to delve into the fascinating history of Gran Canaria.

Outdoor Activities & Adventures

Gran Canaria's diverse landscape offers a playground for outdoor enthusiasts of all levels. From adrenaline-pumping hikes to serene kayaking adventures, there's an activity waiting to awaken your inner explorer. This chapter unlocks some of the most thrilling and rewarding outdoor experiences the island has to offer.

1. Hiking the Tamadaba Natural Park:

- **Activity:** Hiking

- **Location:** Tamadaba Natural Park, accessible from Artenara or other nearby villages.
- **Operating Hours:** Accessible year-round, but weather conditions should be considered.
- **Cost:** Free to enter the park
- **Tips for Beginners:** Opt for shorter, well-marked trails like "La Degollada" or "Presa de los hornos de cal." Wear comfortable hiking shoes, bring plenty of water, and sun protection.

Embrace the lush greenery of the Tamadaba Natural Park on a scenic hike. Explore a network of trails winding through ancient laurel forests, a UNESCO World Heritage Site. Breathe in the fresh mountain air, marvel at the diverse plant life, and keep an eye out for unique bird species like the blue chaffinch and the Berthelot's pipit. Choose from challenging climbs with breathtaking views to shorter, family-friendly paths perfect for a leisurely stroll. Don't forget to pack a picnic lunch to enjoy amidst the tranquility of the forest.

2. Kayaking in Mogán:

- **Activity:** Kayaking
- **Location:** Mogán Port, various kayak rental companies operate in the area.
- **Operating Hours:** Most companies operate from morning to late afternoon.
- **Cost:** €20-€30 per person for a few hours (prices may vary depending on the company and duration)
- **Tips for Beginners:** Choose a guided tour for beginners, as they can provide instruction and ensure safety. Opt for a calm day with minimal waves for a more comfortable experience.

Paddle your way through the crystal-clear waters of Mogán on a kayaking adventure. Explore hidden coves and secluded beaches inaccessible by land. Witness the dramatic coastline from a unique perspective, and marvel at the colorful marine life swimming beneath your kayak. Many companies offer guided tours that combine kayaking with snorkeling, allowing you to explore the underwater world teeming with vibrant fish and coral reefs.

3. Caving in Guayadeque Ravine:

- **Activity:** Guided Caving Tour
- **Location:** Barranco de Guayadeque, various companies offer guided caving tours in the area.
- **Operating Hours:** Tours typically operate during daylight hours.
- **Cost:** €25-€35 per person (prices may vary depending on the company and the duration of the tour)
- **Tips for Beginners:** Choose a reputable company with experienced guides. Wear comfortable clothing and footwear suitable for uneven terrain. A helmet and headlamp will likely be provided by the tour company.

Embark on a subterranean adventure with a guided caving tour through the Guayadeque Ravine. Explore a network of ancient caves carved into the volcanic cliffs, some of which were used as dwellings by the island's indigenous people, the Guanches. Witness fascinating cave paintings and learn about the history and cultural significance of these unique archaeological sites. The tours typically involve some climbing and walking over uneven surfaces, so a moderate level of fitness is recommended.

4. Stand Up Paddleboarding (SUP) in Puerto Rico:

- **Activity:** Stand Up Paddleboarding (SUP)
- **Location:** Puerto Rico, various companies offer SUP rentals and lessons.
- **Operating Hours:** Most companies operate from morning to late afternoon.
- **Cost:** €15-€20 per hour for board rental (lessons may be extra)
- **Tips for Beginners:** Take a beginner lesson to learn the basics of paddling and balance. Choose a calm day with minimal waves for a more stable experience.

Test your balance and enjoy a unique perspective on the coastline with stand-up paddleboarding (SUP) in Puerto Rico. Glide across the turquoise waters on a paddleboard, feeling the gentle sea breeze and soaking up the stunning scenery. SUP is a fantastic way to explore hidden coves and secluded beaches, allowing you to experience the coastline at your own pace.

5. Coasteering in Puerto de las Nieves:

- **Activity:** Coasteering (guided adventure)
- **Location:** Puerto de las Nieves, some companies offer coasteering tours in the area.
- **Operating Hours:** Tours typically operate during daylight hours.
- **Cost:** €50-€70 per person (prices may vary depending on the company and the duration of the tour)
- **Tips for Beginners:** Choose a reputable company with experienced guides. Be comfortable with swimming and basic fitness as the activity involves climbing, jumping, and swimming. A life jacket and helmet will be provided by the tour company.

Coasteering offers a thrilling experience for those seeking an adrenaline rush. Explore the dramatic coastline of Puerto de las Nieves from a unique perspective. Traverse along volcanic rock formations, jump into crystal-clear coves, and swim through hidden tunnels. Coasteering tours typically involve a combination of cliff jumping, swimming, snorkeling, and exploring caves, all under the guidance of experienced instructors. This activity is not for the faint of heart, but for those who embrace adventure, it promises an unforgettable experience.

6. Surfing in Las Canteras Beach:

- **Activity:** Surfing Lessons
- **Location:** Las Canteras Beach, Las Palmas. Surf schools operate along the beach promenade.
- **Operating Hours:** Lessons are typically offered throughout the day, depending on the surf conditions.
- **Cost:** €30-€40 per person for a group lesson (private lessons may be extra)
- **Tips for Beginners:** Take a beginner lesson to learn the fundamentals of surfing, safety protocols, and proper wave selection. Surf schools typically provide all the necessary equipment, including a surfboard and a wetsuit.

Catch a wave and experience the thrill of surfing at Las Canteras Beach in Las Palmas. This popular beach offers consistent waves suitable for surfers of all levels. Learn the basics with a professional instructor, or if you're already a seasoned surfer, challenge yourself on the rolling waves. Las Canteras Beach boasts a vibrant surfing scene, and watching experienced surfers carve through the waves can be an inspiring sight.

7. Scuba Diving in Marine Reserve of Arinaga:

- **Activity:** Scuba Diving (PADI certification required)
- **Location:** Marine Reserve of Arinaga, on the southeast coast of Gran Canaria. Dive centers operate in the area and offer guided dives.
- **Operating Hours:** Dives are typically conducted during daylight hours, with weather conditions being a major factor.
- **Cost:** €60-€80 per person for a guided dive (including equipment rental)
- **Tips for Beginners:** If you're not already certified, consider enrolling in a PADI Open Water Diver course during your trip. This internationally recognized certification allows you to explore the underwater world safely under the supervision of a qualified instructor.

Immerse yourself in the underwater paradise of the Marine Reserve of Arinaga on a scuba diving adventure. This protected area boasts a rich biodiversity of marine life, with vibrant coral reefs, playful fish, and even majestic manta rays and turtles. Explore shipwrecks teeming with life, dive through underwater caves, and witness the wonders of the ocean firsthand. Scuba diving is an unforgettable experience that allows you to connect with the natural world in a profound way.

8. Stargazing at Degollada de la Becerra:

- **Activity:** Stargazing Tour (guided)
- **Location:** Degollada de la Becerra, a mountain pass in the center of Gran Canaria. Many companies offer stargazing tours departing from various resorts.

- **Operating Hours:** Tours typically operate at night, starting a few hours after sunset.
- **Cost:** €20-€30 per person (prices may vary depending on the company and the duration of the tour)
- **Tips for Beginners:** Dress warmly, as temperatures can drop at night, especially at higher altitudes. Bring a blanket or camping chair to sit on comfortably.

Escape the light pollution and marvel at the breathtaking night sky on a stargazing tour at Degollada de la Becerra. This mountain pass offers exceptional visibility, allowing you to see a multitude of stars, planets, and even distant galaxies with the naked eye. Experienced guides will point out constellations, share fascinating facts about astronomy, and answer any questions you may have. This is a unique opportunity to appreciate the vastness of the universe and reconnect with nature's beauty.

Fun Things to Do During Your Visit

Gran Canaria offers a plethora of ways to keep you entertained beyond the iconic sights and sun-drenched beaches. This chapter delves into a variety of experiences that will add a touch of excitement, cultural immersion, and family-friendly fun to your island getaway.

1. Explore the Fascinating World of Aquariums: Poema del Mar and Cocodrilo Park:

- **Location:**
    - Poema del Mar: Puerto Rico de Gran Canaria, Mogán Municipality, Spain
    - Cocodrilo Park: Agüimes, Gran Canaria, Spain
- **Why Visit:**
    - Poema del Mar:** Immerse yourself in the underwater world at Poema del Mar, a stunning aquarium showcasing the diverse

marine life of the Atlantic Ocean and the Pacific Ocean. Marvel at sharks gliding through a massive main tank, witness the vibrant colors of tropical fish in coral reefs, and come face-to-face with fascinating sea creatures like penguins and sea turtles. Interactive exhibits and educational talks provide a deeper understanding of the importance of marine conservation.
  - Cocodrilo Park:** Embark on a thrilling journey through the world of reptiles at Cocodrilo Park. Encounter over 500 crocodiles from various species, including the awe-inspiring Nile crocodile. The park also houses a variety of other reptiles like snakes, lizards, and iguanas. Daily feeding shows offer a glimpse into the fascinating behavior of these creatures. Additionally, a botanical garden allows visitors to explore a diverse collection of plants from around the world.

2. Delve into the History of Arucas Rum: Visit the Arucas Rum Factory:

- **Location:** Arucas, Gran Canaria, Spain (Guided tours require booking in advance)
- **Why Visit:** Step back in time and discover the secrets behind the production of Arucas Rum, a renowned local spirit with a rich history dating back to the 19th century. Embark on a guided tour through the historic factory, learn about the traditional methods of rum production, and witness the fascinating aging process in oak barrels. The tour concludes with a tasting session, allowing you to savor the distinct flavors of Arucas Rum. A gift shop offers the opportunity to purchase bottles of rum as souvenirs.

3. Take a Day Trip to Fuerteventura:

- **Location:** Fuerteventura, Canary Islands, Spain (ferry departs from Puerto Rico de Gran Canaria or Playa del Águila)
- **Why Visit:** Experience the contrasting landscapes and unique charm of Fuerteventura, a neighboring island in the Canaries. A short ferry ride whisks you away to a world of volcanic craters, pristine beaches with golden sand, and charming fishing villages. Explore the volcanic moonscape of

Corralejo Natural Park, relax on the idyllic beaches of Cofete, or delve into the island's history in the quaint town of Betancuria. Day trips typically offer transportation, ferry tickets, and guided tours, making it a convenient and enriching experience.

4. Thrilling Rides and Water Fun at Aqualand Maspalomas:

- **Location:** Campo Internacional Maspalomas, Maspalomas, San Bartolomé de Tirajana, Spain
- **Why Visit:** Indulge in a day of splashtastic fun at Aqualand Maspalomas, a water park perfect for families and thrill-seekers alike. Experience adrenaline-pumping rides like the Boomerang, the Crazy Race, and the Kamikaze. Relax in the lazy river, unwind in a wave pool, or let the little ones enjoy the dedicated children's area. The park also offers a variety of food and beverage options, ensuring a full day of entertainment and refreshment.

5. A Night of Laughter and Entertainment: Drag Shows and Casino Experience:

- **Location:**
    - Drag Shows: Various locations throughout the island, particularly in tourist areas like Playa del Inglés and Puerto Rico.
    - Casinos: Gran Canaria Casino (Las Palmas de Gran Canaria) and Casino Meloneras (Meloneras)
- **Why Visit:**
    - Drag Shows:** Witness the flamboyant and hilarious world of drag entertainment. Gran Canaria boasts a vibrant drag scene, with talented performers offering dazzling costumes, witty humor, and captivating dance routines. Enjoy an evening of laughter and be mesmerized by the dazzling stage presence of the performers.
    - Casinos:** Try your luck and experience the excitement of casino games at Gran Canaria's casinos. Whether you're a seasoned gambler or a curious beginner, the casinos offer a variety of table games and slot machines to cater to all interests. Enjoy a sophisticated atmosphere with live music and upscale dining

options in some casinos. Remember to gamble responsibly and set spending limits beforehand.

6. Learn to Surf or Catch a Wave with Surf Lessons:

- **Location:** Surf schools operate at various beaches across Gran Canaria, with popular spots including Las Canteras Beach (Las Palmas), Playa del Inglés, Maspalomas, and Playa del Cura.
- **Why Visit:** Embrace the island's surfing culture and learn to ride the waves with professional instruction. Surf schools cater to all skill levels, from complete beginners to those wanting to hone their existing skills. Experienced instructors provide personalized guidance, ensuring a safe and enjoyable learning experience. The thrill of catching your first wave or perfecting your technique will leave you with unforgettable memories. Surf schools typically offer surfboard rentals and wetsuits as part of the lesson package.

7. Explore the Depths of the Ocean: Scuba Diving and Snorkeling Adventures:

- **Location:** Diving centers operate at various locations across Gran Canaria, with popular areas including Puerto Rico, Mogán, and Arinaga.
- **Why Visit:** Discover the underwater world teeming with vibrant marine life through scuba diving or snorkeling adventures. Dive into crystal-clear waters and encounter a diverse array of fish, turtles, rays, and other fascinating creatures. Explore underwater shipwrecks, volcanic rock formations, and vibrant coral reefs. Snorkeling offers a fantastic introduction to the underwater world, while scuba diving allows for a deeper exploration for certified divers. Diving centers provide equipment rentals, expert guidance, and ensure safety throughout the experience.

8. Immerse Yourself in Canarian Cuisine: Cooking Class and Food Tour:

- **Location:** Cooking classes and food tours are offered in various locations across Gran Canaria, particularly in major tourist areas like Las Palmas and Puerto Rico.
- **Why Visit:** Go beyond the typical tourist fare and delve into the rich culinary traditions of Gran Canaria. Participate in a cooking class and learn how to prepare traditional Canarian dishes like "papas arrugadas" (wrinkled potatoes), "mojo sauces," "gofio escaldado" (gofio porridge), and fresh seafood specialties. Under the guidance of a local chef, you'll gain hands-on experience and discover the secrets behind these flavorful dishes. Food tours, on the other hand, take you on a delicious journey through local markets and restaurants, allowing you to sample a variety of Canarian delicacies and learn about the island's culinary history.

9. Stargazing Adventure:

- **Location:** Designated stargazing locations away from light pollution, often in the mountains. Tours typically depart from various resorts across the island.
- **Why Visit:** Escape the city lights and marvel at the breathtaking spectacle of the night sky on a stargazing adventure. Guided tours take you to designated locations with minimal light pollution, providing the perfect conditions for observing the stars, planets, and other celestial objects. Knowledgeable guides will point out constellations, share fascinating facts about astronomy, and answer any questions you may have. Many tours offer telescopes for a closer look at the universe's wonders. Remember to dress warmly for evenings in the mountains.

10. A Journey Through Time: Visit Historical Sites and Museums:

- **Location:** Historical sites and museums are scattered across Gran Canaria, with some notable examples including:

- **Cueva Pintada Museum and Archaeological Site (Gáldar):** Explore a network of ancient caves adorned with pre-Hispanic paintings by the Guanches, the island's indigenous people.
- **Vegueta Historic Quarter (Las Palmas):** Wander through the charming cobbled streets of Las Palmas' historic center, admiring colonial architecture and iconic landmarks like the Santa Ana Cathedral.
- **Canary Museum (Las Palmas):** Delve into the island's rich history and cultural heritage through archaeological artifacts, traditional clothing, and exhibits showcasing the evolution of Gran Canarian society.

- **Why Visit:** Immerse yourself in Gran Canaria's fascinating past by visiting historical sites and museums. Step back in time and discover the island's indigenous culture, colonial period, and the evolution of its society. These sites offer valuable insights into the island's unique character and traditions.

Part 7: Practical Information for a Smooth Journey

Safety and Security Considerations

Gran Canaria beckons you to explore with reckless abandon. But before you dive headfirst into adventure, let's talk about staying safe and secure throughout your island escape. Here are some essential tips I've gathered from my own experiences and from fellow travelers to ensure your Gran Canarian adventure is worry-free and unforgettable.

Sun Sense is Essential: The Canary Islands boast year-round sunshine, but that doesn't mean you can skip the sunscreen. Pack a high-SPF, broad-spectrum sunscreen and reapply generously throughout the day, especially after swimming or sweating. Remember, the sun can be deceiving, so shade your head with a hat and seek refuge under an umbrella during peak sun hours (typically between 11 am and 4 pm).

Respect the Ocean's Power: Gran Canaria's pristine beaches and turquoise waters are irresistible, but always prioritize safety when venturing into the ocean. Be aware of rip currents, especially on less-frequented beaches. If you're unsure about the conditions, don't hesitate to ask lifeguards for advice. When swimming, stay within designated areas and avoid swimming alone.

Embrace Responsible Hiking: Hiking trails offer breathtaking views and a chance to connect with nature, but a little preparation goes a long way. Choose a trail that matches your fitness level and wear comfortable, sturdy shoes. Pack plenty of water, especially during hotter months, and consider bringing snacks for longer hikes. Always let someone know your planned route and estimated return time, and don't stray from the marked paths. Be mindful of the weather conditions and avoid hiking during thunderstorms or when strong winds are forecast.

Be Street Smart: While Gran Canaria is generally safe, petty theft can occur, particularly in crowded areas. Keep your valuables secure, don't leave belongings unattended on the beach, and avoid carrying large sums of cash. Invest in a money belt or a crossbody bag that keeps your essentials close to your body. Be aware of your surroundings, especially at night, and avoid walking alone in poorly lit areas.

Respect Local Customs: Gran Canaria is a place of rich culture and tradition. Dress modestly when visiting religious sites, and refrain from taking photos in places where it's prohibited. Be mindful of noise levels, especially in residential areas. Learn a few basic Spanish phrases to show respect and enhance your interactions with the locals.

Embrace Travel Insurance: Unexpected situations can arise, so consider purchasing travel insurance before your trip. This can provide peace of mind and cover medical emergencies, trip cancellations, or lost luggage.

Download Emergency Apps: Having access to emergency information on your phone can be a lifesaver. Download the local emergency number (112) and consider apps that translate languages or provide medical advice.

By following these simple yet crucial safety tips, you can explore Gran Canaria with confidence, ensuring that your memories are filled with exhilarating adventures, cultural discoveries, and the warm spirit of the island. Remember, a little preparation goes a long way in transforming your trip into a truly remarkable experience. Now, go forth, explore, and create unforgettable memories in Gran Canaria!

Transportation & Getting Around

Gran Canaria beckons you to explore its diverse landscapes, from the bustling capital of Las Palmas to the secluded coves hidden along the dramatic coastline. But getting around this beautiful island can feel daunting at first. Fear not, fellow adventurer! This chapter equips you with all the knowledge you need to navigate Gran Canaria like a local, ensuring your island adventure is smooth sailing (or should I say, smooth driving?).

1. Public Buses:

My first Gran Canaria exploration was fueled by guaguas, the affectionate nickname for Gran Canaria's public buses. These bright turquoise buses are a fantastic way to experience the island on a budget. The network is extensive, connecting major towns, villages, and popular tourist destinations. Downloading a handy bus app or grabbing a local timetable will become your best friend. Pro tip: While hopping off at iconic landmarks is a must, don't be afraid to venture off the beaten path. A spontaneous bus ride to a lesser-known village might just unveil a hidden gem, like a charming local market or a secluded beach.

Sure, buses aren't the fastest option, but that's part of the charm. You'll share the ride with friendly locals, witness the ever-changing scenery unfold outside the window, and maybe even pick up a few basic Spanish phrases from eavesdropping on conversations. Think of it as a cultural immersion on wheels!

2. Taxis:

Sometimes, especially after a long day of hiking or soaking up the sun on the beach, the thought of squeezing onto a crowded bus might be less than appealing. That's where taxis come in handy. Taxis are readily available in most tourist areas and can be hailed on the street or ordered through a phone app. They're a convenient option for late-night excursions or quick trips between destinations not well-connected by bus.

Remember, taxis operate on a meter, so you won't be surprised by hidden charges. However, be aware that fares can add up quickly for longer distances. Having a basic understanding of Spanish can be helpful when communicating with taxi drivers, but most will have some knowledge of English.

3. Car Rentals:

For the ultimate in flexibility and freedom, renting a car is the way to go. Gran Canaria's well-maintained roads make exploring a breeze. Imagine this: you can wake up, grab some fresh pastries from a local bakery, and set off on a spontaneous adventure to a secluded viewpoint or a hidden beach, all at your own pace. Car rentals are readily available at the airport and in most tourist resorts.

While navigating unfamiliar roads might seem intimidating at first, don't worry! Invest in a good offline map or download a reliable GPS app. Many car rental companies offer vehicles with built-in navigation systems for added ease. Remember, driving in Gran Canaria involves mountain roads with switchbacks and occasional roundabouts. Take it slow, enjoy the scenic drives, and be extra cautious on narrower roads.

The Final Choice:

Ultimately, the best mode of transportation depends on your travel style and budget. Buses are a fantastic budget-friendly option for exploring at a leisurely pace. Taxis offer convenience and comfort for shorter distances or late-night outings. And car rentals unlock the ultimate freedom to explore the island at your own pace, venturing off the beaten path and creating unforgettable memories.

Money Matters and Currency Exchange

But before you pack your swimsuit and sunscreen, let's talk about the nitty-gritty: money matters. Don't worry, it's not all spreadsheets and confusing exchange rates. Here's a friendly guide to navigating the financial side of your Gran Canaria adventure, ensuring you can focus on soaking up the sun and good vibes.

The Local Currency:

Imagine strolling through a bustling market in Las Palmas, the capital city. You spot a beautiful handmade ceramic bowl – the perfect souvenir! But hold on, what kind of money do you need? The good news is, Gran Canaria, like all of Spain, uses the Euro (€). So, if you're coming from most European countries, you're already set!

Exchanging Your Cash:

Now, if you're arriving with a different currency, like US dollars or British pounds, you'll need to exchange them for Euros. There are a few ways to do this:

- island, ATMs offer the most flexibility and often have competitive rates. Just be sure to check with your bank beforehand about any international transaction fees.

My personal tip? I usually withdraw some cash at the airport for immediate needs (like a taxi or a quick bite) and then rely on ATMs for the rest of the trip.

Carrying Cash vs. Cards:

While Gran Canaria is becoming increasingly card-friendly, especially in tourist areas, carrying some cash is still a good idea. Small shops, cafes tucked away in charming villages, and local markets might only accept cash. It's also handy for tipping and paying for public transportation tickets.

Tipping Etiquette:

Tipping in Gran Canaria is not mandatory, but it's always appreciated. Here's a general guideline:

- **Restaurants:** A small tip of 5-10% of the bill is customary, especially if you received excellent service.
- **Taxis:** Rounding up the fare is a common practice.

- **Hotels:** Leaving a small tip for housekeeping staff is a nice gesture.

Remember, a friendly smile and a "gracias" (thank you) go a long way in Gran Canaria, regardless of tipping.

Planning Your Budget:

Now, let's talk about budgeting. Gran Canaria caters to a range of budgets. Here's a rough estimate to get you started:

- **Budget-friendly:** €50-€75 per day
- **Mid-range:** €75-€125 per day
- **Luxury:** €125+ per day

This can vary depending on your spending habits, accommodation choices, and activities. But with a little planning, you can have a fantastic time in Gran Canaria without breaking the bank.

Final Thoughts:

Managing your money on vacation shouldn't be stressful. With a little preparation and this guide in mind, you can navigate Gran Canaria's financial landscape with ease. Now, go forth, explore, and make amazing memories on this beautiful island!

Emergency Contact Numbers

Planning a trip is exciting, but it's always wise to be prepared for anything. Imagine you're having a fantastic time on Gran Canaria, soaking up the sun on a beautiful beach. Suddenly, you realize you misplaced your wallet, or maybe a minor sunburn feels worse than expected. Don't worry, these things happen! To ensure a smooth and stress-free vacation, here's a list of essential contact numbers you might need during your Gran Canaria adventure:

Emergency Services:

- **112:** This is the **universal emergency number** in Gran Canaria. Remember this number! In case of a medical emergency, fire, or police assistance, dial 112 and a multi-lingual operator will connect you to the appropriate service. **Stay calm and speak clearly** when explaining the situation.

Tourist Assistance:

- **+34 928 22 68 00:** This is the phone number for the **Gran Canaria Tourist Board**. If you encounter any difficulties or have general questions about the island, this is a great resource. Multi-lingual staff can assist you with anything from finding a lost item to recommending restaurants or attractions.

Medical Assistance:

- **+34 928 41 20 00:** This is the general number for **Hospital Doctor Negrín**, the main public hospital in Las Palmas de Gran Canaria. Hopefully, you won't need it, but it's good to know in case of a medical emergency. Most tourist resorts have local medical centers with English-speaking staff who can assess minor ailments or provide referrals to specialists if needed.

Police:

- **091 (National Police):** If you experience theft or require police assistance, dial 091. The National Police handle most situations, and some officers may speak basic English.
- **062 (Guardia Civil):** The Guardia Civil is another police force with a presence in Gran Canaria. Dial 062 if you encounter issues outside major towns or cities.

Additional Resources:

- **British Consulate (Las Palmas):** +34 928 36 22 00 (if you're a British citizen)
- **US Consulate (Las Palmas):** +34 928 43 40 00 (if you're a US citizen)
- **Travel Insurance:** Double-check your travel insurance policy and make note of their emergency contact number. This can be invaluable if you require medical treatment or lose important documents.

Keeping a copy of these numbers handy (written down or saved on your phone) can provide peace of mind during your trip. Remember, most people in Gran Canaria's tourist areas understand basic English, so communication shouldn't be a major hurdle. However, having a basic Spanish phrasebook can be helpful in certain situations.

Here's a pro tip: If you lose your phone or wallet, the first thing you should do is contact your accommodation provider. They might be able to help you retrace your steps or connect you with local authorities.

Tourist Traps to Avoid (tips for navigating scams and maximizing your travel budget)

Let's face it, paradise doesn't come cheap. But that doesn't mean you have to break the bank to have an amazing experience in Gran Canaria! I've been there, done that, and learned a few things along the way – some the hard way, of course. I'm here to help you avoid the tourist traps and navigate the island like a seasoned traveler, maximizing your budget and memories.

The Pricey Pushers:

- **Restaurant Rip-Offs:** Those picture-perfect menus with mouthwatering descriptions right on the main strip? They might look tempting, but be cautious. These restaurants often cater to tourists with inflated prices and mediocre food. Instead, wander a few streets back from the beachfront. Local restaurants frequented by Canarians will offer delicious, authentic cuisine at a fraction of the price. Look for places with daily specials or "menús del día" (set menus) for a budget-friendly lunch option.

My Experience: I once fell victim to a beachfront restaurant with a charming waiter who promised "the freshest seafood in Gran Canaria." The seafood was decent, but the bill made me wince. Next time, I ventured into a little side street and found a hidden gem of a restaurant – friendly staff, delicious local dishes, and a bill that left me smiling.

- **"Free" Activities with Hidden Costs:** Beware of flyers promoting "free" cultural events or demonstrations. These often lead you to shops or presentations where the "sales pitch" can be quite intense. If something sounds too good to be true, it probably is. Do your research and choose reputable companies for paid tours or activities.

My Money-Saving Trick: Instead of those "free" demonstrations, I stumbled upon a local festival by accident. The streets were alive with music, dancing, and delicious food stalls. It was a truly authentic experience that cost me next to nothing.

Taxis and Transportation:

- **Taxi Tricks:** Taxis are a convenient option, but they can add up quickly. Download a ride-hailing app like Cabify or Uber, which often offer more competitive fares. For short distances, consider the well-connected public bus network. Tickets are affordable, and you get to experience local life while traveling.

My Budget Hack: I discovered the local buses are not only cheap but efficient. Plus, it's a great way to practice my Spanish with fellow passengers!

- **Car Rental Conundrums:** Rental car deals might seem enticing, but factor in hidden costs like fuel, parking fees, and additional insurance. If you're staying in a central location with good public transportation or plan to relax on the beach most days, a rental car might not be necessary. However, if you want the freedom to explore remote areas, compare rental companies and avoid impulse decisions at the airport.

My Money-Saving Maneuver: I opted for the public buses for most of my trip. For one day trip to a remote village, I split the cost of a rental car with another traveler I met at my hostel, making it much more affordable.

Shopping Savvy:

- **Souvenir Switcheroo:** The souvenir shops on the tourist strip are full of mass-produced trinkets. Seek out local markets and artisan shops for unique handcrafted souvenirs. Haggling is acceptable at some markets, but do so politely and respectfully.

My Souvenir Score: I found a charming market tucked away in a side street. After a fun haggling session with a friendly vendor, I walked away with a beautiful, locally made necklace as a souvenir.

- **Beach Chair Bonanza:** Renting sunbeds and umbrellas on the beach can be expensive, especially if you plan to spend a lot of time at the beach. Consider buying an inexpensive beach umbrella or mat for the duration of your trip.

My Beach Bum Bliss: I invested in a lightweight beach mat and saved a significant amount compared to renting sunbeds every day. Plus, having my own mat meant I could find a more secluded spot on the beach for some peace and quiet.

Remember:

- **Do your research:** Read reviews of restaurants and activities before you go.
- **Ask locals for recommendations:** They'll know the hidden gems and budget-friendly options.
- **Pack versatile clothing:** You can mix and match outfits to avoid overpacking and needing to buy extra clothes.
- **Embrace the local way of life:** Travel at a slower pace, enjoy the scenery, and avoid the urge to rush through every attraction.

Conclusion

As the sun dips below the horizon, casting a warm glow across the rippling waves, a bittersweet feeling washes over you. Your Gran Canaria adventure is nearing its end, but the memories you've collected will stay with you long after you return home.

Remember that exhilarating hike through the Tamadaba Natural Park, the scent of pine filling your lungs as you marveled at the ancient laurel forests? Or perhaps the thrill of kayaking in Mogán, the turquoise water lapping against your kayak as you explored hidden coves and vibrant marine life.

The taste of fresh seafood enjoyed on a charming harborside restaurant terrace, the laughter shared with loved ones during a lively festival, the sense of wonder while discovering the island's hidden gems - these are the moments that will find a special place in your memory box.

Gran Canaria has a way of weaving itself into the fabric of your being. It's not just the postcard-perfect beaches or the dramatic volcanic landscapes; it's the warmth of the people, the rich cultural tapestry, and the endless possibilities for adventure.

As you pack your bags, a tiny piece of Gran Canaria might find its way in - a bag of locally roasted coffee beans to remind you of energizing mornings, a piece of handcrafted Canarian jewelry as a reminder of the island's artistic spirit, or maybe a jar of the island's signature "mojo" sauce, ready to transport you back to those delicious meals.

But the most precious souvenirs you'll take home are intangible. It's the newfound sense of adventure you discovered, the ability to find joy in the simple things like a breathtaking sunset or a starlit night sky. It's the deeper connection with nature you forged, the appreciation for different cultures you embraced, and the unforgettable memories you created with loved ones.

So, as you bid farewell to Gran Canaria, know that a part of you will always remain on this enchanting island. And who knows, maybe someday you'll return, ready to discover new hidden gems, create more cherished memories, and fall in love with Gran Canaria all over again.

Printed in Great Britain
by Amazon